OTHER BOOKS BY LESLIE LEYLAND FIELDS

Forgiving Our Fathers and Mothers:
Finding Freedom from Hurt and Hate

Hooked!: True Stories of Perseverance, Death, and Love from
Alaska's Commercial Fishermen and Women

The Spirit of Food: 34 Writers on Feasting and Fasting toward God

"Parenting Is Your Highest Calling" . . . and Eight Other Myths
That Trap Us in Worry and Guilt

Surprise Child: Finding Hope in Unexpected Pregnancy

Surviving the Island of Grace:
Life on the Wild Edge of America

Out on the Deep Blue: Women, Men,
and the Oceans They Fish

The Entangling Net: Alaska's Commercial Fishing Women
Tell Their Lives

The Water Under Fish (poetry)

I have friends whose nearly every thought is filtered through their academic life, and others for whom the world of sports shapes most of their conversations. With Leslie Leyland Fields, like Jesus, we encounter someone whose life floats into memoir through the world of water, wind, and waves as well as fish, boats, and storms. In the hands of Leslie's very able pen, a life of family fishing in Alaska slides into a sacrament that opens up the life of Jesus, the Gospels, and the life of Jesus' disciples. Jesus, with an insider's wink, would like her stories.

SCOT McKNIGHT
Author of *A Fellowship of Differents*, *Kingdom Conspiracy*, and *Sermon on the Mount*

Leslie Leyland Fields invites us into what at first glance is a life most of us will never experience. However, her experience couldn't be more relatable to readers as she navigates the transition of midlife, the bittersweet ache of an emptying nest, and her questions about what it means to follow Jesus here and now. *Crossing the Waters* carries us across time and culture, netting fresh insight into the disciples' journey.

MICHELLE VAN LOON
Author of *Moments & Days: How Our Holy Celebrations Shape Our Faith*

This book is a rare gift. It pulses with story and theology, with lived suffering and quiet joy, with vast mysteries and a strong Savior. The question is not whether you can put it down— because that will be hard—but whether you have the good sense first to pick it up, and read.

MARK GALLI
Editor in chief, *Christianity Today*

In *Crossing the Waters*, Leslie Leyland Fields takes us on a spiritual journey that leads us across the world—from the island in Alaska she calls home to the Holy Land, where she sails the

Sea of Galilee—and across time, where we fish alongside the earliest followers of Jesus. Through it all, she paints a vivid portrait of faithful endurance.

TREVIN WAX

Managing editor of The Gospel Project, author of *Clear Winter Nights: A Journey into Truth, Doubt, and What Comes After* and *Counterfeit Gospels*

The disciples could often be found battling rough seas, storms, and empty nets. As an Alaskan fisherman for nearly four decades, Leslie Leyland Fields brings unique insight to the disciples' experiences with Jesus—and how we, too, can learn to trust and follow the Savior.

JIM DALY

President of Focus on the Family

Before reading *Crossing the Waters*, I didn't yet realize that the guide I most needed to steer me through turbulent waters was one whose hands smell of finger kelp. With insight, wisdom, and a deep connection to the maritime world from which Jesus plucked his first followers, Leslie Leyland Fields blesses readers who want to see the Word, and see Jesus, with fresh eyes.

MARGOT STARBUCK

Speaker and author of *The Girl in the Orange Dress*

Like the seas she and her family fish in, Leslie Leyland Fields's *Crossing the Waters* is challenging, changing, crisp, bracing, beautiful, sometimes dangerous, and teeming with life. A wonderful storyteller, she invites us into her life and in so doing brings Bible characters to life as real flesh and blood, sweat and stink, spirit and grace people called to follow Jesus. This book is a gift!

J. BRENT BILL

Minister, photographer, retreat leader, and author of *Holy Silence: The Gift of Quaker Spirituality* and *Life Lessons from a Bad Quaker*

What can a group of first-century Middle Eastern fishermen teach a twenty-first century Alaskan fisherwoman? Just about everything that really matters. Recasting her own enchanting but gritty life in the commercial fishing industry alongside those "fishers of men," Leslie Leyland Fields shows us how each of our life stories is best understood in light of the "good story," the gospel.

KAREN SWALLOW PRIOR
Author of *Booked: Literature in the Soul of Me* and *Fierce Convictions—The Extraordinary Life of Hannah More: Poet, Reformer, Abolitionist*

Set in the stormy waters of Alaska and on the Sea of Galilee, this beautiful, challenging, uplifting book by Leslie Leyland Fields gives us context for the teachings of Jesus. Fields's life has not been easy, and she does not pretend that any of us will sail smoothly through our own experiences. Instead, she opens her life as a mother, daughter, spouse, and friend, and exposes her personal challenges as she applies the teachings of Jesus. As she hikes through Israel, Fields uses her knowledge of fishing in Alaska to put Scripture into context. An inspiring book for personal or group study, *Crossing the Waters* offers unique insight and inspiration.

DALE HANSON BOURKE
Speaker and author of *Embracing Your Second Calling* and The Skeptic's Guide series

FOLLOWING JESUS
THROUGH THE STORMS, THE FISH,
THE DOUBT, AND THE SEAS

Crossing the waters

LESLIE LEYLAND FIELDS

NAVPRESS⊙.

A NavPress resource published in alliance
with Tyndale House Publishers, Inc.

NavPress is the publishing ministry of The Navigators, an international Christian organization and leader in personal spiritual development. NavPress is committed to helping people grow spiritually and enjoy lives of meaning and hope through personal and group resources that are biblically rooted, culturally relevant, and highly practical.

For more information, visit www.NavPress.com.

Crossing the Waters: Following Jesus through the Storms, the Fish, the Doubt, and the Seas

Copyright © 2016 by Leslie Leyland Fields. All rights reserved.

A NavPress resource published in alliance with Tyndale House Publishers, Inc.

NAVPRESS and the NAVPRESS logo are registered trademarks of NavPress, The Navigators, Colorado Springs, CO. *TYNDALE* is a registered trademark of Tyndale House Publishers, Inc. Absence of ® in connection with marks of NavPress or other parties does not indicate an absence of registration of those marks.

The Team:
Don Pape, Publisher
Caitlyn Carlson, Acquisitions Editor
Mark Anthony Lane II, Designer

Cover photograph copyright © Kevin Carden/Lightstock. All rights reserved.

Author photo by Jessica Davis Photography, copyright © 2016. All rights reserved.

The author is represented by the literary agency of WordServe Literary, www.wordserveliterary.com.

Some of the anecdotal illustrations in this book are true to life and are included with the permission of the persons involved. Some names have been changed to protect privacy. All other illustrations are composites of real situations, and any resemblance to people living or dead is purely coincidental.

Cataloging-in-Publication Data is available.

ISBN 978-1-63146-602-1

Printed in the United States of America

24	23	22	21	20	19	18
8	7	6	5	4	3	

To my readers,
who are always generous,
whose words and lives inspire me
to follow closer.

CONTENTS

ACKNOWLEDGMENTS

IN THIS UPSIDE-DOWN WORLD of writing books, it is always the acknowledgments that are written last. It makes some kind of sense. We don't know who to thank until we finish. (In fact, for many months, sometimes even years, we do not even know *if* we will finish.) By the time we get there, the list of enablers, readers, and suppliers (of chocolate and encouragement) has multiplied like loaves and fishes. I only hope I have fed others as much as they have fed me along the way.

Grateful thanks to three particularly astute readers: Michelle Novak, whose mind and heart spark often into godly brilliance; my pastor, Peter Sprague, who read every chapter and offered comment and encouragement; and Heather Johnson, who has relentlessly cheered me onward.

The kind, smart women of the Lake Michigan Writer's Workshop gave excellent input on the title and heard the first pages of this work. Your responses grew my faith.

Special gratitude to the people of my church, Community Baptist Church in Kodiak, Alaska, for bearing with me through the reading and teaching of early forms of each chapter, and for sharing stories from your own lives among fish and water. You all mean more to me than I can say.

Greg Johnson has continually offered hopeful words and wise counsel for many years now. I'm blessed to call you agent and friend.

All the people at NavPress have been incredible to work with. This book wouldn't exist without Don Pape's enthusiastic support. My editor, Caitlyn Carlson, has been amazing in her acuity and patience with me. The prayers of the whole team for me and for these words during the crucible of this last year truly kept me going. You are living examples of discipleship.

And what shall I say to my family? They're long used to a wife and a mother who cares more about the structure of a sentence and the narrative arc of a book than the cleanliness of the kitchen floor. But I want you to know it is your love that has awakened my heart to love for the world.

Most of all, I thank the One who has remained faithful through all my doubts and wanderings. Whatever light glimmers from these pages comes from you.

INTRODUCTION

"LESLIE, can you take the skiff back to the island?" Duncan asks.

All the crewmen on the beach—seven—turn and look at me skeptically. I scan the ocean one more time. My island is just two miles away, but the waters are a tempest of urgent, roiling waves. The wind has come down since morning, but it's still blowing about thirty miles per hour. It's not far to go, but half of the distance I will travel will be climbing the waves skyward and then skittering down the other side. The trick is to keep the boat quartered in the waves, and to stay away from the curl and break. No one wants to travel in weather like this, especially in an open twenty-six-foot skiff, not much more than a rowboat. I know how to do it. I've run plenty of boats in nasty weather, but anxiety sweeps my insides.

"Sure, I can do that," I say coolly. I have to go. My son Noah, twenty-three, is taking one skiff back, and they need someone to take the other. I've spent the whole day working on this other island, and if I don't go now, I'll be stuck here overnight with nowhere to sleep—an unpleasant prospect.

I pull up the hood of my orange rain gear against the wind,

tighten it, strap on my life jacket, cinch it, trying to look and feel nonchalant, strong. As if I am not dwarfed by the crewmen around me, men less than half my age and twice my size. As if I will not be dwarfed by those hissing seas. Even by the skiff itself. I stand in the stern, pulling my five-foot-two inches as erect as I can while the men launch me from a trailer. The long aluminum boat groans and slides into the water while eight men, all in the same orange rain gear I am wearing, push me off and watch. As soon as the water is deep enough, I let down the sixty-horsepower outboard, start it, and reverse slowly from the protected eddies.

For the first ten seconds, the water is calm enough. Then it begins. The full force of the wind catches my hood. Spray lashes my face. Each wave that lumbers across from the open ocean moves like a whale about to breach. I watch every curl, try to keep the bow angled just right. When my skiff swells upward, I see Noah a half mile ahead of me, his skiff rising and disappearing between waves, like mine. I stand taut in the boat like a single muscle. My face is awash in seawater. The ocean roars in my ears. I am scared, but I know I will be home soon.

These are the waters we cross every day. We commercial fish for salmon every summer here on this island, a one-mile mountain of green, rock, and dirt in the Gulf of Alaska, off Kodiak Island. In my better moments, whether I'm riding a wild sea, mending net on shore, or out fishing in the boats, I feel almost biblical here. I remember the stormy sea crossings of the disciples. I feel a special connection to those men fishing and washing their nets two thousand years ago by the Sea of Galilee. With a mix of astonishment and pride, I remember that Jesus chose fishermen as his very first disciples, and Peter was chief of them all! Yes, I feel it—this life on the shoreline, on the water, in the storms, has grown my faith immensely. Though I have had numerous reasons to leave, I am still here, thirty-eight years later. This fishing life has not been easy. And following Jesus in the midst of it has been confusing and difficult. I still have so many questions. What does it really mean to "follow Jesus"? (Jesus called those fishermen away from the nets, and I am still here!) And, even more fundamental, who *is* Jesus, anyway? What is his claim on my life? What is his claim on *all* of our lives?

I tell you honestly, in the middle of my life, in the middle of *this* life—I have a lot of questions that I want answers for. But more than answers, I need to see Jesus again. I need to hear him again. I am guessing you need this as well. I am more than guessing. I have met so many who have left their faith, who have left the church, who have given up on the Bible, who have "unfollowed" Jesus. I know you have too. Clearly, many are struggling with their faith, with the church, with Jesus himself.

We wonder, too, about relevance. How can what happened two thousand years ago in a tiny Middle Eastern country matter to us now? How can the short life of a Jewish rabbi who died too soon have any claim on my life? And we're busy. We're tired, with too many burdens and distractions: children, work, elderly parents, health issues, careers.

Even those of us who are sure we are followers of Jesus, we have issues too! We've read the Gospels countless times. We've heard about Jesus' miracles in more Sunday school lessons and sermons than we care to recall. We can instantly extract a moral lesson from any of the parables and miracles. We've got it down. The suspense is gone. The surprise is gone. We know how it all turns out. Yawn. And then when we do wake up, we're sodden with guilt and failure. What kind of "followers" are we, anyway?

We know we haven't "taken up our cross" to follow him each day. We know we've slipped into apathy and fatigue. We know we're not living up to what God requires: to love him with all of our heart, our mind, our soul, our strength.[1]

We need to go again, then, all of us. One more time. We need to enter into the story of Jesus with expectant eyes, with open ears, because these stories are the truest ever told. Nothing has more power to awaken and shake and shape us than these accounts and encounters with Jesus. This trip through the Gospels will be different than others. It's an immersive on-the-ground, in-the-water experience, just as it should be because the Gospels are anything but dry. They are dramatic, wild—and wet, set in a rich maritime culture on the shores of the Sea of Galilee. I understand something about this world; it's not so far from my own. In the midst of all these waters and words and worlds, I've been brought startlingly near to this man who claimed to be God. I want to bring you closer to see and experience for yourself.

We're looking as well for the *human* stories we have missed, the story of twelve men whom we have too easily scooped up, cleaned off, and served up merely as Bible messages, minus the messiness of real people, real fishermen—equally at home with their families and their doubts, their zeal, and their unbelief. These raw stories of the gospel will lead us more surely to whatever and whoever might be divine in the events and waters they splash around in. These stories can help us decide who we are, and whether we want to follow this man Jesus—or not.

So here's where we're going. Think of it as one giant float trip. I'll take you from whatever field, city, or neighborhood you live in, and we'll cross to my Alaskan waters. We'll ride through a season of commercial fishing in this wild corner of the world. I want you to see, smell, and taste the waters here as I (try to) follow Jesus. We'll cross the waters to Israel as well, where I hiked the "Gospel Trail" around the Sea of Galilee and went out fishing with Galilean fishermen. And we'll step out on a new journey through the Gospels, dipping into some of the wettest, stormiest, strangest events of those three years.

"Come, follow me," Jesus beckoned to the astonished fishermen, and he beckons to us as well all these centuries later. We'll follow him, then, through those waters: the Jordan River, where he sank under river waters and rose like a dove; and the shores of the Sea of Galilee, where he strode atop the waves of a storm, broke two small fish into a feast for thousands, filled a net to breaking when no fish could be found, shouted down a storm from a sinking boat. Where he fed his friends a meal of grilled fish, commanding "feed my sheep" . . . before disappearing into heaven. I promise you a trip unlike any other.

But I have to warn you. Travel is risky, especially in Alaska, and especially in the Gospels. Storms come up, you have only oars against the sea, there are too many in the boat, everyone argues, and you can't keep the water out. Will we get to the other side safely, our minds clearer, our eyes and ears fixed on Jesus? I'm as nervous as you are as I step into the boat because I know there will be fear, high seas, and spume along the way. Maybe even some whales will breach beside us. But I also know what came after those crossings—people were healed, parties broke out, the sightless walked straight, the starving ate fish that never ran out, and twelve common men (finally) grew confident and fearless.

Maybe some of this will happen for us as well.

CHAPTER ONE

THE GATHERING OF THE WATERS

And the Spirit of God was hovering over the face of the waters.
. . . And God said, "Let the waters under the heavens be gathered together into one place, and let the dry land appear." And it was so. God called the dry land Earth, and the waters that were gathered together he called Seas. And God saw that it was good.

GENESIS 1:2, 9-10, ESV

It's May 28. Our summer begins. We're flying out from our house in Kodiak perched over the ocean to our fish camp surrounded by ocean. We're not thinking about this, of course—that our lives are divided between two islands, and the water joins them both, and the water separates them both. Do we think of the air as we breathe it?

I am flying out with my two youngest sons, Abraham and Micah, thirteen and eleven in this summer of 2014, and my assistant for the summer, Kristi. I crouch in behind them and let Kristi sit up front next to the pilot. The boys climb into the back seats of the bush plane, a six-seater. It's a wheel plane, which means if there's any reason during the flight we need to make an emergency landing, we're sunk. There's no level ground on this island crossing. Just ragged mountains. Sometimes we charter a floatplane and land on our front waters, our own beach, stepping out in knee boots, from plane to water to shore. This is the best. Should we need to drop from the sky for a crash landing, there's a water runway everywhere.

"Got your seat belts there?" the pilot asks, a young, fresh-faced guy.

The boys strap in, arguing over who gets to hold Sophie, our Yorkie. I check to make sure Kristi is fine with sitting shotgun. She shoots an excited smile back at me. I don't even remember that, the excitement of a first bush plane flight.

The engines rumble. In a minute we are taxiing off and then we're up over the ocean, banking west. I watch the rise over the water, the canneries, the container ships towed in from a vast ocean by a tugboat, and within seconds we are lost in a sea of snowed mountains. It's the end of May, but the snow will remain for a while. The hills and town itself will be green in another week or two. But it's the water I see most. Though we are crossing the interior of the second-largest island in the United States, there is almost nowhere that water can't be seen. The deep fjord-like bays reach long, craggy fingers to massage the heart of the island. It is these two together, mountains and ocean, that have come to define beauty for me.

It is not a long journey across Kodiak Island to the island we live on and commercial fish from every summer. We fly sixty-five miles across to the village of Larsen Bay, population 50 in the winter, about 350 in the summer, counting the cannery workers. We land bumpily on a gravel airstrip, unfold our bodies, and crouch onto the wing, then jump to the dirt to help the pilot unload our 350 pounds of goods, each box weighed on a scale and marked. I am glad to see the van from the cannery, our ride down to our skiff.

My son Elisha, eighteen, is there at the cannery store in his full orange rain gear, our summer uniforms, sucking an ice cream cone when we arrive. He's been out here a month already, getting gear ready. I see he's started some kind of beard. The boys and I jump out of the van, take turns hugging Elisha and stealing bites from his ice cream. We unload the boxes from the van to the beach, then into the twenty-six-foot open aluminum skiff, our main summer transport, which will take us on a seven-mile pounding ride to our island. The whole journey is not even a hundred miles, and we don't change a single latitude, but our life here is a world apart from our life in town.

Though the trip this year has gone easily so far, travel in this country is often complicated. I remember a trip we made out on a larger boat, traveling the twelve hours through a stormy night, with not enough bunks for all. My son Isaac slept on the galley floor, rolling from side to side. Noah tried to sleep on a galley bench. I spent half the trip out gulping fresh air on the slick deck to keep from vomiting. Other times we take our own boat, the *Cowboy*, a pudgy scow, good for carrying freight but worthless in any seas, rolling like a tub. In my early years here, we took a twenty-five-foot speedboat, until one September when we were caught in huge seas, taking on waves that nearly sank us. It was our second close call with that boat. We sold it soon after.

The day after I make it here, when my husband, Duncan, tries to fly out, the weather has turned bad. The bush plane, a Beaver, takes off anyway and makes it to Port Lions but has to land because the fog is so thick. Then something goes wrong with the plane. It is grounded by a mechanical issue, then flies back to Kodiak for another try the next day.

My daughter, Naphtali, twenty-five, and my brother-in-law are coming out to the island the next day on a thirty-two-foot boat. They leave Kodiak at midnight and will travel all night around the stormy waters of Kodiak Island, the sea still swelling with the remains of a forty-mile-per-hour northeastern blow. They'll stay alert, awake, eyes on the sonar to avoid treacherous reefs along the way. When they arrive in the morning, they'll suppress their exhaustion and join the others to put out the fishing nets all afternoon.

Isaac, twenty-one, is coming for the first month only, before leaving to continue his chemistry research with a professor in California. Noah is coming for a short visit, then it's back to California, his girlfriend, and the new job he just landed. It's the first summer he's not returned to work. I wonder if he'll ever come back.

Tonight, though, I will curl up alone in my bed on my faraway island where no one lives but us, the island I have finally come to love. I will pray for them, for my daughter, my only daughter out on a big sea in a very small boat. I will ask Jesus to keep them safe. I will ask for Duncan's safe arrival by bush plane. I feel guilty sometimes always asking for this, as if safety is our right. But I keep asking anyway, In three weeks I will be praying for my brother-in-law and nephew, who will take that same thirty-two-foot boat a thousand miles along the desolate waters of the Alaska Peninsula to fish for red salmon in Bristol Bay.

I will pray, too, for this season on the water ahead of us. I remember the year my daughter was seventeen, her third year running her own boat. After just nine days of fishing, she stood there in the doorway in all of her rain gear, her hair in a bandana, her hands clenching at her sides. "I can't do this," she said, looking at me in despair. "I can't do another season." I looked back at her sadly, knowing how hard the last few years had been, the onslaught of salmon, the grueling weeks with little sleep, the swollen fingers. My children returned to school and college barely able to hold a pencil.

There have been years, too, when I didn't want to come back, but I did. We all did. We are still here, on the nets, in the boats, on the water, in a life encircled by salmon, who themselves are returning to die.

What is this life I have been given? Or did I choose it? Didn't I come here following Jesus? Or following my new husband? Or both? After all these years, this is what I know for sure: This is not a safe life for either body or soul. Just gathering all of us now into this fishing life is itself a sailing, and every summer this island drifts into deep, complicated waters.

Just hours after we land and load and unload our dozens of boxes of supplies from the beach up the steep hill to the house, I see a furious splashing out by the reef in front of our house. A pod of orcas hunting down sea lions? "Micah! Abraham! Come quick!" They run to the window with me, watching strange flippers emerge, then a huge dark body leaping out of the water.

"What is it?" the boys ask together. Then I know.

"It's a pod of fin whales. They're lunge feeding!" My eyes are fixated on their antics. I almost can't believe it. Fin whales are sober whales. They don't cavort or frolic like humpbacks. They're massive, second only to the blue whale, and they haul their heft with great solemnity about the oceans. They know what life is about. They migrate to this bay again and again every summer, like me. They've seen it all.

But now—there are fresh herring darting into the bay. Now it is nearly summer. Now they give up their old habits and indulge in what's called lunge feeding. I've read about it but never seen it. They're feeding on their sides, skimming and scooping up schools of herring, their usually invisible flippers flapping and slapping the water. We watch with binoculars as they rise and roll, flushing the waters with their spinning and lunging, mixing water and whale and air into a wondrous froth. Why merely sink and dive when they can spin and skim their seventy-ton bodies up onto the lovely surface and net whole schools of tasty fish? And there we are, laughing, witnessing their perfect feast, and who knows what else is possible in this watery world?

All the next day my steps are light with joy. I remember
G. K. Chesterton's words:

> It is possible that God says every morning, "Do it
> again" to the sun; and every evening, "Do it again"
> to the moon. It may not be automatic necessity that
> makes all daisies alike; it may be that God makes every
> daisy separately, but has never gotten tired of making
> them. It may be that He has the eternal appetite of
> infancy; for we have sinned and grown old, and our
> Father is younger than we.[1]

Is it possible that already I am young again, full of hope
for the season ahead? The waters that threaten us, that wear
us out and down, also inspire and launch the world's heaviest
creatures into the air—can it be? But it is. And I think again
of the gathering of waters, the *mikveh*, the Hebrew word for
that moment in Genesis when God called out all the waters
above and below into a single massive body, the seas. The same
word, *mikveh* (literally meaning "collection"), came to be used
of every gathering of water that cleansed and purified. A convert
to Judaism would immerse himself into the *mikveh*, a special
pool of water for that very purpose, waters that were sometimes
called "the womb of the world." As the convert came up out of
the waters, he emerged new, as a child, now separated from his
own pagan past. He was called "a little child just born," or "a
child of one day."[2]

I am a "child of one day" this day, the spume of the whale
washing over me. I am converted from the wear of age and
time and so many trips and seasons and fear and doubt out

here—made young again by delight. And it is easy to think of God creating the oceans right now. It is easy to think of Jesus right now. So many times I am looking for him, for that man who has rescued me in such particular ways, and who remains yet so far off, so invisible that I am blinded with longing and frustration. Other times, now, he feels so present around these waters that I cannot contain it. I know it is no accident. Water saturates the Scriptures, from the Spirit hovering over the waters, to the Holy City of Revelation and the river flooding its streets, and so many places in between: streams in the desert, water from the rock, the well of living water, the *mikveh*, the gathering of the waters.

Out of nothing came water and land, came our ocean and island. Every year, my children and I launch off blindly in tiny planes or boats to return to our land and sea. And no matter how thick the fog or how high the seas, I swallow my worry and choose to believe we will arrive, that the months ahead will be fruitful, that all of us gathered around the table, gathered by the waters, will see and name all that lies ahead, finally, *good*.

CHAPTER TWO

UNDER THE WATERS

In those days Jesus came from Nazareth of Galilee and was baptized by John in the Jordan.

MARK 1:9, ESV

It is June 9. The fishing season began four days ago with a northeast wind blowing forty knots. It is still blowing, the cold wind snatching away the start of our summer. The men, including two of my sons, set the fishing nets out in the storm, in seas too heavy for open twenty-six-foot skiffs. They have done this all their lives—they've suffered many storms—but in such wind, it is always harrowing. After four days of it, they are exhausted, fighting six-foot waves equipped only with their own arms and a sixty-horsepower engine. They are in now from a morning at war on the water.

It's lunchtime. Everyone is in from the nets, with one more trip to the nets coming later in the evening, after a rest. We sit at the table, eight of us, eating broiled king salmon, the season's first. I sit at the head. Duncan is in Nome all this week. Four of my sons and two crewmen and Kristi sit here with us. The fishermen's hair is curled and crusted with salt water.

"I had a dream last night," Elisha begins. "I was in the skiff traveling up this huge wave. The wave never ended, and I just kept on going forward, higher and higher."

"Was I in the skiff with you?" asks Peter, twenty-three, the crewman who works in the bow of the skiff while Elisha runs the motor in the stern.

"Yeah you were!" Elisha laughs, mouth full of potatoes. "You were scared to death, and you kept telling me to turn around. But I knew if I turned we'd flip over. I didn't know what to do. I was so scared!" He laughs again.

We all laugh, and the conversation turns to falling in, to falling out. The mood is merry inside while the wind whistles over the roof outside. *Remember when Paul leaned too far over to catch a line and he went over headfirst, smooth as a seal, right into the water? Remember when two crewmen loaded the skiff too heavy and swamped it right there at the net? They got to shore by pulling themselves in with the corkline of the net.* I have my own stories to add: when my daughter Naphtali, at fifteen, out in a big blow, was snatched from her perch on the tote into the foaming sea. I think of another storm years ago, when the kids were younger. It was howling, gusting fifty miles per hour, the seas a heaving riot. We no longer go out in such weather, but we did then.

I went out in that storm that day to the fishing nets with all the men. We dressed carefully as we prepped to go out into the blow. We pulled our caps lower over our eyes, snapped up our rain gear to our chins against the pummeling waves, zipped up our life jackets. I said a prayer as we pounded out to the straining nets, barely able to see for the spray, the wind, our stomachs in knots, our senses all alert. The waves came at us in eight-foot fists.

Three of us sat hunched on the seat in the stern, trying to stay low. "Get on the floor!" Duncan screamed over the wind after a wave nearly knocked us sideways. We were sitting too high for these waves. They could sweep us out in a single swipe. We dropped to the floor of the skiff, which was already swilled in seawater. It took us twenty minutes instead of five to get to the nets, and once there, we couldn't even get close to them for the breaking sea. We hung on for the long, violent ride back, to find quieter nets with more protected waters.

At a fish camp not far from ours, three people in boots and full rain gear, the same as us, jumped into a skiff bucking in the high surf on the beach. Two, husband and wife, were not wearing life jackets. They were from the tropics, and had worked on the water a long time in all kinds of weather, but always warm weather with the ocean always bathtub warm. They did not fear the water. As their boat lurched out, wave by wave toward the nets, the skiff took too many waves, overturned, and the husband and wife were in the water, in frigid water too stirred for swimming—or breathing. Floating was possible with a life jacket, but it was too late for that.

Alaska waters are not tropical waters. If we don't understand where we are, the dangers and realities of the place we are living, if we are not awake to the water and sky around us, we will miss living well. We might even die.

Our own stories at the table don't last too long. Like most fishermen, we have a lot of close-call stories, but not a lot of fall-in-the-water stories. One of the chief aims in fishing in Alaska is staying out of the water. Mostly we do. In my first year of fishing, when I went out with Duncan to put out the nets, it was my job to clear the net of tangles as it flew out the stern, the skiff moving fast as we went. I knew if my boot caught in the spiraling net I'd be pulled over in a flash. I would dream of drowning, sunk by my heavy boots and rain gear, caught in the lead line of the net, dragged to the bottom. Most anyone who lives and works out here, whose life is circumscribed by the water, has at least dreamed themselves drowning at the bottom of the sea. It is not baptism unless we survive, and most of us do, though we are never the same.

My first fall into these waters came thirty-eight years ago, the year I flew up to see Duncan, to try on this life, like a boot, to see if it fit. We were engaged to be married in a year, and we both knew I needed to see what I was choosing. I was not choosing just a man; I was choosing a place, an island, a life of work, and a particular piece of ocean that would lap at my feet the rest of my days.

Nineteen years old, my black hair hanging to my hips in a single braid, I stood at the edge of the dock in a T-shirt and shorts, ready to jump. Duncan had already jumped, screaming as he sprang up toward breath and sun. It was not swimming weather by my New Hampshire body, but here in this new country, sixty-five degrees was warm enough to leap into a cold sea, wasn't it? Of course I would jump. Hadn't I flown all the way up here from New Hampshire by myself, my first flight ever? Wasn't I ready to leave my old life behind to live in this brilliant seascape of whales and boats and fish? I smothered the flutters in my stomach, took one last breath, kicked out from the dock, knifed out, into and under water that snatched me down to the grave. I rose screaming too, breathing ice then fire, my own body and breath saying, on rising, *I will. I do.*

In another country, another time, across the wide ocean, a man stands in water. It's wilderness there, too, but a different kind: it's desert wild, with unrelenting sun and heat, a place without soil, softness, or fertility of any kind, where you suffer from thirst and dearth. But there is a river. That's where he is, this loner wrapped in a tunic woven of camel hair, with a leather belt around his waist, who survives on insects and honey robbed from the comb. The kind of man, like all the prophets, who sees too much, who glimpses what's to come, who must shout about it. And it's never good news. "Repent!" he yells, like all the others, one chosen messenger after another through their whole history, sorry men all, bellowing about their wickedness and rebellion against their God, about the judgments that were coming. It always came true, in every bitter detail, as if the words of the prophets themselves made it happen. But it has been so long since they've heard these words, or any words from God at all.

"Repent!" comes this call in the desert, again and again, his words breaking a four-hundred-year silence. *Repent!* The few out there who are listening wait, cringing for the next words about judgment—don't they know they're living under it right now, under these pagan Romans? They know about Roman judgment firsthand. Wasn't their own city, Sepphoris, just three miles from Nazareth, burned to the ground and thousands of their people sold into slavery just a few years ago? Surely that was judgment from their God. And now this fellow. Of course there will be warnings about fire, capture, and enslavement—isn't this the history of their people? But they hear something else. "The kingdom of heaven is coming!" he shouts again and again.

The Kingdom of Heaven is coming? Now, at last, after all these generations, the Kingdom of Heaven—and it is coming now, to us? A few families come to hear these words from the man by the river, then more come, in small groups and pairs, until now his shouts and words are heard by whole villages of people clustered on the riverbanks. Is this Elijah, they wonder, this man who is dressed like him, who speaks like him? People are believing him, believing that something is finally about to happen, and they want to be part of it. They are tired of their old lives. Tired of their failures, tired of waiting for a deliverer who has not come these thousand years. Tired of hoping God will come back to them and live with them again, as he did once, back when he first called them to be his people. Hasn't he promised this? That he would live with them again? That his Kingdom would "reign from sea to sea"?[1] That he would "cut off . . . the war horse from

Jerusalem," that prisoners would be "set . . . free from the water-less pit,"[2] that Jerusalem again would be called "the Faithful City"?[3] They know the words of the ancient Scriptures.

And is it now finally coming, what God has promised? They are not sure, but this man, he seems sure. Others have come before him—calling themselves Rescuer, Deliverer, King! Those who came announced themselves as the One! But this man is different. Look, how open his face and how direct his eyes! Hear the strength of his voice and words! Some know he is speaking from one of the ancient scrolls, Isaiah. When the river-gatherers ask him, "Who are you, so that we may give an answer to those who sent us? What do you say about yourself?" John answers straight from the prophecy that told of his coming: "I am a voice of one crying in the wilderness, 'Make straight the way of the LORD!'"[4] He is the only one who has come saying, "I am *not* the One!" No one has ever seen or heard a man like this.

The men and women are so full of hope and so empty with themselves and their defeated people, they follow him out into the river. Of course they had to come here, to the Jordan. They were wanderers in the desert until they crossed this river. When their ancestors stepped into its waters, it happened again—just like at the Red Sea. The water gathered together, a *mikveh*. It heaped up in a wall, like a wave rising higher and higher, and did not break. With dry feet on the sandy bottom, they crossed, the whole throng, two million of them under that unbreaking wave. When they emerged on the other side of the Jordan, and the waters rushed back into place, they were home. They were born anew. They were children again. Were they surprised?

Though they had just come through forty years of desert

nomading, they knew about water, the floods that covered the earth before it was made. They knew about the gathering of the waters into one place for the genesis of life. Yet after all was made, "Every inclination of the thoughts of the human heart was only evil all the time"[5]—so the *mikveh* was released again, now to drown the world and all its life. One family, though, was saved through those waters to begin anew in a world washed clean.

They know about water, these children of Israel watching the prophet. Don't they wash and purify themselves before the Day of Atonement, before they eat, and a dozen other times a week? They know about going under water. It brought them life. It delivered them, and in its cleansing, it reminds them of all the ways they have failed.

Here, then, they come and pour it out to him, this baptizing man. Before they sink under the water, they spill it all out—how they have stopped waiting for God, how they have stolen from their neighbors, how they have cheated their overseers, how they have grown tired of clinging to words scrawled on a scroll, how they have made an idol, how they have stopped going to synagogue, how they have given up teaching their children. They have never spoken these words to anyone before, and how is it now these words come spouting out of them like this?

It's almost a circus out here, with so much crying and river-splashing and dunking. There are shouts and pronouncements, people hugging each other in their wet robes. People daring to believe that maybe it is beginning now, their release from their oppressors! The return of God to his people! How many generations have recited these words from Isaiah's scroll? "The LORD has anointed me to proclaim good news to the poor. He has sent me to bind up the brokenhearted, to proclaim freedom for the captives and release from darkness for the prisoners."[6] They feel clean for the first time in their lives.

And into this hullabaloo one day strides a man, a quiet man who passes and presses through the crowds. But he is not invisible. The Baptizer sees him, hitches his breath, and points his own circle of men to the other side of the river—"Look, there he is, that's him . . ." They look. They cannot see at first for all the other robed men, but then the tip of John's finger catches a face, and he finishes, "That's him, the Lamb of God who will take away all the sin of the world."[7]

This strange man comes toward them until he is face to face with John. The two embrace while the others look on, amazed. The "lamb" speaks something to John, and John pulls back, stricken. "No! How can this be?" The quiet man speaks again. He slowly nods, and in a moment, the men and women standing near watch it happen. The same as the prophet has done for them. The Baptizer takes a deep breath and places his hands, his rough desert hands long gone soft in so much water, on this man's head, and pushes him under. He is down for three full counts, longer than the others, and finally he rises, exploding out of the river with a shout—and is that a laugh? And some laugh with him. Until they see it, something falling from the sky, flittering, swooping like a bird. All eyes follow, now silent. Where is it going? Maybe into the water—isn't this holy water already? Or onto the Baptizer? But it falls—onto him, or into him, the man just risen from the water. It falls into him and disappears. They are still openmouthed when, from the same sky, thunder booms—or is it a voice? And they hear these words: "This is my much-loved Son. I take delight in him."[8] (Did anyone see it, the Creation story again? God hovering over the new waters of the world, speaking his delight in them, and now, too, hovering over the waters, declaring his joy in his Son?)

Here at this river, the man God has just named "my much-loved Son" stands there in a pool of water, every inch soaked in the *mikveh* that began the world that birthed their nation.

Was there ever such a time of hope and beginnings?

And somehow that beginning, that man rising from that river, even the beginning of all the beginnings, has something to do with all of us, wherever we are.

A few months after the fishing season, I go to the Jordan River to see for myself. It is November 17, the first day of my hike around the Sea of Galilee. Noah and I are going to walk from Tiberius to Yardenit, a ten-mile trek up a thousand feet to the hillside, through the Swiss Forest and the high country there. Then, as we near the south end of the lake, we'll descend and land somewhere near Yardenit, the place on the Jordan River where people gather for baptisms.

Yardenit is famous. Most pilgrims come here to be baptized in the same waters that Jesus went under. I did my research before I left. I know the name comes from *yarden*, meaning "descent."[9] The river begins up on the slopes of Mount Hermon, about 1,800 feet above sea level. By the time it empties first into the Sea of Galilee, then into the Dead Sea, this small river ends at the lowest place on the planet, at 1,410 feet below sea level.[10]

I have been to the baptismal site twice before some thirty years ago, but I have little memory of it. How could I have forgotten such an important place? But in some ways, I don't want to go again. The river has not fared well in the two thousand years since Jesus was here—even in the thirty since I was last here. My reading delivers only bad news. Agricultural pesticides drain from the surrounding hills into its waters. Raw sewage from hotels is dumped into the lake on its shores. The saline levels are climbing. The water levels are controlled to the very gallon, with a large percentage of the freshwater diverted to Syria and Jordan. The Six-Day War, in fact, was fought over the control of these waters. The river has become so dirty in this last decade that environmental groups have attempted to shut down the two baptism sites on the Jordan because of its unsafe levels of pollutants. Holy waters indeed.

The day of hiking is going well, better than I expected. I am delighted to find that the trail, though hard to find, is empty. We see no other hikers the whole day. No one at all, in fact, except for two passing cars. We are quite alone, which gives us the chance to walk in silence. I cannot shake the wonder that I am here now in Israel, standing over the waters of the Sea of Galilee instead of at home in Kodiak, on a cliff by the ocean, huddled under winter storms and thinking about Thanksgiving, my son Micah's birthday, all the events of a November at home. Sometimes it is easier than we think to interrupt our own lives.

Three hours into our walk, we take a lunch break in a grove of bushes beside an empty road. We bought pita bread and hummus from a corner grocery store on our way out of Tiberias. We eat it now, sitting in the dirt, in the scant shade, with appetite and gratitude. It has been a hard haul for me, still adjusting to eighty-degree heat, carrying a thirty-pound backpack up the climb to the plateau we are on now. Between eager bites, I suddenly hear a "whoosh!" from below us. We stand and turn reflexively, to the lake below us, eyes searching before we remember. I laugh. "I thought it was a whale."

"Me too!" Noah says.

It's hard for me to remember that the Sea of Galilee is not a true sea at all. It's a freshwater lake. In this first day of the walk, I realize I am disappointed. The usual temperature for this time of year is fifty, sixty degrees, which would have been perfect for my Alaska body thermometer. The heat has summoned a thick haze above the water and the surrounding hills and mountains. I cannot see clearly. I expect beauty and clarity from water. But if there is beauty here, it is muted. And the trail is poorly marked and hard to find. I wonder if I will find my way around the lake, especially without Noah. We spent the previous week together exploring Jerusalem, and we'll hike together again tomorrow, but the next day he returns to the States to his job. I know I'll miss him on the rest of the hike, but I'm grateful for the week we've had together.

After lunch, we descend from the hilltops and hit level ground, which makes walking easier, but the trail seems to disappear entirely. We give up looking for it and beat and bushwhack our way across fields, leaping over canals. Our quarry now is the river—or, even better, the hotel we've booked for the night, the only hotel near the baptismal site. There are a few campgrounds around the sea, but they are all closed. Just about the time I am fantasizing about ice cream and worrying about the coming dark, we stumble out of a freshly plowed field to face the sign for the hotel. "Noah! We're there!" I shout in amazement. It feels like a miracle.

I intended to go to the baptism site the next morning, but

I can't wait. After checking in, dumping our backpacks, and downing a cold drink, Noah and I follow the receptionist's pointed finger down the road. We cross the busy highway, my steps now increasing. Before I can even see the river I hear singing. Then the parking lot—with fleets of tour buses, cars. I walk through the entrance of a low, nondescript building, but around the entrance are tiles written in every language I have heard of and ones I haven't. The entrance takes me through the gift shop (of course), then out again—into a party. Two hundred people, I guess, many dressed in white robes, mill and clump, some strung along the railings over the river itself. Somewhere a choir is singing and clapping. Above the guitars and praise music, someone shouts, "Praise Jesus!"

I angle slowly to the railing and find an empty spot between a man perhaps from Africa and an Eastern Orthodox woman. Where is the singing coming from? Where is the river?

And there it is, a sludgy green pond small enough to pole-vault across. It is as sad as I anticipated. My heart sinks. But the river is hardly dead. Despite the massive algae growth and its own turpitude, it is alive with bodies. Aeration is clearly coming from the people in the river, not the river itself. But no one seems to notice or care that this is a dying river. Least of all the ones standing in the river itself.

One group holds everyone's attention. Dressed in the white robes, which I discovered could be rented for ten dollars apiece, fifty dark-skinned men and women clap and sing in four-part harmony with energy and rich-throated beauty. They dance, moving rhythmically to the guitar music at the water's edge. One by one they wade out to their two pastors, who put their hands on each head, speak, then dunk them backward under the water. Every one follows the same pattern. They rise, their faces erased for a moment, then they wobble and faint. Men in white robes catch them and carry their slain-in-the-Spirit bodies slowly like the dead, lengthwise, up the steps to lay them down beside the ones before them.

What is this swoon? Swallowed by the water that swallowed up Jesus, what do they see? I feel a deep stirring. Should I, too, rent a robe and drop under the river? Duncan asked me before I left, "Are you going to get rebaptized?" I was aghast at his question. "Of course not! I am not one of *them*." I am not sure who the *them* was. Perhaps these people here before me now, these joyous clapping singing swooning people? Am I not one of them?

I was baptized at seventeen in the Suncook River, a slow, silty river that curved through the mill town I went to high school in. My pastor was there, and others from my youth group. My parents were not. I was wearing a white robe, and I walked out into the water like these Yardenit pilgrims, and dunked under, and it was done. No one was singing. I did not faint or swoon or see heaven open, but I was asking for just as much. I wanted my old life and my old heart washed away. I lived in a house without heat, without a future, without hope. I died in that house a long time ago, until I heard of this man Jesus. He saved my life. I would follow him, I decided, even into the river. Dripping with brown river water, I was starting life again—with him. I was no longer alone.

But that was forty years ago. What could I claim since then, that I had lived this wondrous life of faith and joy and obedience to this Savior? Maybe I need to do it again. Maybe I'll see heaven open or feel God's Spirit overtake me. Maybe I can find it, get it here—more of God. Maybe this is my chance! I stand by the river's edge, paralyzed with indecision. I don't even see the two women beside me until they speak.

"Would you take our photo standing in the river?" The women, in red, look hopeful.

"Sure!" I smile, glad for the interruption. "Where are you from?"

"Ghana."

"Wow, that's wonderful!"

They hand me their camera, a pocket-sized digital. We find an empty piece of river beach. "How about there?" The women, middle-aged and maybe sisters, step into the brackish water.

"Oeeeuuww, that's cold!" they squeal, rolling up their jeans further.

I'm angling with the camera but can't get the composition just right. "Can you take one more step out so I can get more of the river?"

"Ohhh no, it's too cold!"

We all laugh, and I snap a few of them beaming, heads together, feet in the water.

"Where do you fellowship?" they ask me when I am done.

"In Kodiak, Alaska."

"No, what kind of church?"

I think a minute, then decide to keep it simple. "I go to a Baptist church."

"Oh, I am Methodist!" says one of the women.

"I am Presbyterian!"

"All part of the body of Christ!" I say, giving the first my arm as she steps out of the river.

"Oh yes indeed!" she answers back, the other adding, "Amen,

sister!" behind her. We grin at each other like conspirators before we turn away.

Warmed by this encounter, I look for others to speak to. Over by a kiosk, I see a group, Hutterites from Europe, perhaps, standing rapt, watching a video. I come as close as I dare to see what they are watching. A rhapsody of violins accompany a man with a chinstrap beard and a blunt bowl haircut, draped in the white rented robes, wading chest deep into the green river, dunked, rising, an exultant smile, and then on to the next, a woman, her long white hair unpinned. I realize finally that they are watching a video of themselves, and discover soon after that this is a service the place offers. You can buy a DVD of your baptism for fifteen dollars. There it is, forever preserved, the moment captured. You cannot forget.

I stand near a young man with the same bowl haircut, and wearing brown trousers and vest, clearly homemade. His demeanor is gentle and inviting.

"Hello," I venture, not even knowing if he speaks English. He turns away from the video to look at me with surprise. "May I ask, where are you from?"

"The US," he answers back, with an American accent.

I am the one surprised now. "Where in the US?"

"I'm from Ohio. Others in my group are from Montana, Indiana, all over."

"You are—"

"Amish," he finishes.

"Yes." I nod. And suddenly I'm conscious that I'm in dirty black shorts and a tight, sweaty tank top. This would not be my chosen attire for a meet-the-Amish session. But he doesn't seem to notice.

"Where are you from?" he asks.

"Alaska."

"Alaska! Really?"

And we begin talking, until soon his smartphone is out (*Are you allowed to have those?* I am thinking). I marvel over the photos of his seven children, who are age fourteen down to one, and I show him photos of my six. Finally I ask what I really want to know. "Why are you here?" and I gesture to the river, the crowds, the video.

He smiles patiently. "This is our fourth time in Israel. We're here on a mission of forgiveness and reconciliation with the Jewish people."

I look at him, puzzled. "Forgiveness for whom?"

"Us! We looked at our history and recognized that we had blamed the Jewish people for the death of Jesus. We had not supported them or understood them. We've spoken against them in our own communities. We've been wrong." His green eyes looked at me steadily.

Some Brazilians are singing and clapping, I hear splashing and laughing, but it all falls away before this man.

"How do you go about this?"

"We come to meet with rabbis and other leaders to offer our repentance and ask for forgiveness. We are building bridges between our two communities, realizing how much we share in common."

"That's amazing," I stammer. "I've been studying a lot about forgiveness myself." I tell him about the book on forgiveness that I have just finished writing. It is not long before he introduces me to others in his group, to four pastors, all wearing the same haircut, but two of them in black suit coats.

We talk for a long time about what God is doing in the Amish community. "Signs and wonders," one pastor tells me. "God is pouring out his Spirit on our people. Thirty years ago, most Amish did not know the Lord Jesus personally. There was a lot of legalism, a lot of rule-making and rule-keeping, but few of us had a relationship with the living God. That's all changing now."

When we finish, we clasp each other's hands. I hold on too long, not wanting to let go. I turn from this conversation, walk through a group of Koreans, while a busload of Africans wearing batik collect at the river. Every tongue and tribe is here today it seems. I cannot stop trembling.

I see one spot open on a bench near the railings. Overwhelmed, I sit down next to a seventyish man dressed all in white. He is putting his socks and shoes back on. Another river-wader, I think. We begin to talk. He is off a cruise ship in the Mediterranean, he tells me. They are in Israel just two days. I try to place his accent. Then he tells me. He is German, from Saskatchewan. In just seconds, he confesses to me, "I don't beleef in any of this hocus-pocus." He waves his hand as the praise music fills our ears. "It's ridiculous. How can there be a god? What are you going to tell me about Hitler, eh? And the tsunami that killed all those people. No, with that kind of evil, there's no god. I beleef in the stars."

I listen, mildly surprised at first, but I shake my head in sympathy as he speaks. *Of course, these are big questions.* Perhaps I should say more, but I don't feel a need to evangelize or engage in apologetics here and now. I remember what happened those many years ago, that even then in the midst of all the waterworks of new birth, others stood at the edges of the river, at

the edges of the rejoicing and shouting. The Sadducees and
Pharisees were there, glowering, doubting, suspicious. Who was
this man daring to act like some kind of prophet? What kind
of audacity was this, to dress like a madman and announce the
arrival of "the kingdom of heaven"?

John's response to them is shocking, not what I would have
scripted for the messenger of God. There's his voice again,
shouting at the dark-robed figures on the bank, "You brood
of vipers! Who warned you to flee from the coming wrath?"[11]
They are angry, of course. They feel fear rising in their throats.
What is this power they see breaking out among the people?
All these people under the river, out under the sky—not inside
the synagogue, under their authority, where they belong. So
it begins already, before we hear even a word from Jesus: the
threat of heaven. And I remember this: Not all who follow, not
all who gather at the river go under the water. Some follow to
gape and carp. Some follow to destroy. Others are not even following, only standing on the edges to watch. They're not sure
about John. Even less sure about this One to come. They have
waited so long, it is hard to stop waiting. They don't even like
the water. They are like us—they need to see more.

It is not so different now. Now I see others here who are
clearly tourists, with fancy cameras and long lenses, or with
straw hats from the cruise ship. A few are positioned on the railings, gaping at the spectacle, their cameras aimed at the baptizers. An older man dressed in beige looks down on the baptizers
with disdain. I watch a man and a woman, perhaps from the
Philippines, carry five-dollar plastic jugs from the gift store into
the river, filling them with the brown water to take back home.
Maybe they'll sell it or use it for baptisms in their own church.

27

Out beyond the barrier in the river, where no one is allowed, a group of teenagers and adults are hooting and cannonballing off a boulder. A small man by the video kiosk nervously breaks off an entire branch of an olive tree and hands it quickly to two women, who guiltily look for a place to hide it. I am suddenly very tired. As I leave, the gift shop is shoulder to shoulder with people lined up to buy holy oils from Jerusalem, a crown of thorns, a vial of holy dirt from the riverbank, Christmas ornaments. Salesmen hover, offering "special prices."

What a world this river has made!

An obscure man whom people knew only as a carpenter from a nearby village, itself known for nothing, walked the shores of this unremarkable river and submitted himself to a loony man in animal skin to be shoved under water—and two thousand years later, churches, families, tribes from all nations still come across continents to fall into these waters, waters nearly killed by politics, agriculture, and economics. Yet still they come to confess, to sink, to rise, to swoon, to watch, believing that all can be cleansed under this water, that reconciliation between enemies is possible, that foreigners can be made a family, that no matter what they've done, God will forgive them. There are even benches here for unbelief.

What is the power of this water and this place? And is it only present in this river and the Sea that feeds it? No. The Jewish people consider the ocean also as a *mikveh*, the very first gathering of the waters, and so, too, holy in some way.

Half a world away, we stumble in from our salt water, drenched, fatigued, but we keep going back, we keep launching our boats onto and under the waters. And I will come back to this river, I decide, when the hike is over. I must come back.

Maybe after hiking all the way around the lake I will want to be baptized again.

What do I know as I leave this place?

I don't know all that happened that day almost two thousand years ago when the much-loved Son burst from those waters, and a piece of heaven ripped wide, but I do know this from my own sea and from this river:

Wherever there is water, the thirsty and the dirty are there.

Once you go under the water, you're never the same.

CHAPTER THREE

CALLING OUT
OF WATER

As Jesus was walking beside the Sea of Galilee, he saw two brothers, Simon called Peter and his brother Andrew. They were casting a net into the lake, for they were fishermen. "Come, follow me," Jesus said, "and I will send you out to fish for people." At once they left their nets and followed him.

Going on from there, he saw two other brothers, James son of Zebedee and his brother John. They were in a boat with their father Zebedee, preparing their nets. Jesus called them, and immediately they left the boat and their father and followed him.

MATTHEW 4:18-22

WE'RE TWO WEEKS INTO THE FISHING SEASON. Nothing but storms and rain. I'm waiting for the weather to break so I can go out in the skiff with my sons. This night the northeast wind has finally settled. I know there's still a big swell down on Seven-mile Beach, where half of our nets are, but the nets around our island should be calmer. "Can I go out with you tonight, Elisha?"

"Sure." He shrugs. I did not expect enthusiasm.

"How about if Micah comes with us too?"

Elisha is always up for time around Micah. Micah is the youngest, born on my forty-fifth birthday. While he's never been babied, he still attracts the delight and attention of all his older siblings. He's translated this into a wry wit.

I round up my gear, which takes a few minutes. I haven't been out since last year, and of course my things are scattered. My XtraTuf knee boots are right by the door. I finally find my new rain pants, exactly the color of halibut backs—a murky black-green—and my raincoat, finally one that fits! I've used the same ones the men use all these years, heavy-grade neon orange Grundéns, but they're always too big and flop around me like a sail. This year I have a child's large, and the sleeves fall just to my fingers. I am pleased. I cannot believe I have waited all these years to buy gear that fits. I grab a life jacket from the gear shed, pull on rubber gloves with long plastic sleeves that go up to the forearm, and then finally add the last layer, cotton gloves over the rubber gloves for gripping the slick salmon. As a bonus, the gloves add a further layer of insulation against the cold waters.

Elisha and Micah, who are out on the nets most of the day, are ready before me, waiting at the skiff. I've not fished with

Elisha since I don't know when. I am not any of my sons' preferred bowman, being of lesser weight, strength, and length than their usual crew, all of whom are in their twenties. Long arms and weight-lifting biceps are a decided advantage when leaning out of the skiff to snatch the corkline and pull it up into the boat, all while in motion. But I'm agile and experienced.

We're picking the Harvester nets, my favorites—not just because they're local, the nets off our own island, but because they take us to the dark back side of the island where the steep dramatic cliffs drop straight to the ocean. On one end, the slate cliff face has crumbled in an earthquake and landslide, leaving jagged spires and shattered rock. Here, it feels the earth is ending—or maybe just beginning.

Elisha's skiff is the same as the rest in our fleet of skiffs, a twenty-six-foot aluminum boat, a sleek flat-bottom craft that can run up on the beaches for comings and goings. It's as personal as a tin can to me—each skiff bears not a name but a number—but to the boys, who virtually live in their skiffs for the summer, it's a kind of home. They know its every corner and weld.

It's a quick run to the first net, which is anchored out not far from my writing studio. Each day as I sit and write in my new studio, my desk set up under windows over the bay, I watch the skiffs zip past. I am chasing words and choosing sentences; they are chasing fish and picking kelp. Both jobs are hard. But tonight I'm the one in the skiff skimming the water past my studio. I am swapping words about fish for fish themselves, a glad and overdue trade. I don't want to think about words, about chapters, about a book. I just want to work, get wet, handle fish, be with my sons.

We arrive at the first net. Elisha slows and turns the skiff sideways so Micah and I can lean over, grab the corkline, and pull the net into the boat. Our nets are set gill nets—stationery, attached to shore. We are the ones that move. From a chain or a heavy poly line, the nets extend out into the water in a more or less straight line, depending on how hard the tide is running. The last half of the net ends in a diamond shape. The diamond-shaped meshes are designed to be just the right size to catch a fish trying to pass through. Our work is to raise the net from the water to set it in a roller in the bow, and as the net passes before us, to extract every salmon from its entanglement, something that can be done in experienced hands in as little as two seconds—or sometimes the fish is so tangled it can take two minutes.

Micah and I are in the bow, leaning over the railing, ready to grab. No one talks. There's no need to. I reach down into the water and grasp the corkline and jerk it upward. Micah grabs the line with me and together we hoist it up and into the skiff.

"Good job, Micah."

We begin to pull the net toward us, pulling toward the lead line that keeps the net sunk. It's a good night to be out, I am thinking. I get tired of being on shore, where there is nowhere to travel for a change of scenery except a few short hikes. While the ground is alive with grasses and flowers I am always bending to see, the water feels so much more expansive. It's our roadway, open to many possible destinations.

When we pull the lead line up, we set the whole net in the skiff and will run it down the length of the boat, with the sixty-horsepower engine idling us slowly down the net. Micah and I stand at the ready to pick fish, kelp, whatever the net delivers to our hands. There are few fish here tonight, I see as we go. Five minutes in, a strange brown body appears.

"A pouty fish!" Micah exclaims happily. He is always delighted when entertainment shows up, in any form.

I look at it closely. "It's a lumpsucker," I correct him.

"We call them pouty fish," he says definitively. And since they are out on the water all the time and I am not, I let it stand, though I believe in calling the things of this world their proper names.

"Take a picture, Mom," Elisha says. "I've always wanted a photo of a pouty fish, but I never take my camera out."

"Pouty fish photo session coming up!" It's a huge risk taking a camera out in the skiff on a pick, but I've done it this time. It is a necessary part of seeing this world anew.

The boys each pose with the lumpsucker, which is nothing more than a fish that's all face and head, without a body. The impoverished lumpsucker's main feature, besides its malevolent, grumpy expression, is a giant suction cup under its belly where it latches on the bottom surface, waiting for jellyfish or mollusks to happen by.

We snap a few, with Elisha holding the lumpsucker up beside his face, mugging a grump to match the fish's mien. Micah holds the fish beside his face as well, smiling, and with his free hand, pushing the unfortunate fish's lips into a mirroring smile. We laugh. And we are off again, now motoring more quickly through the net to make up for lost time. We've got a lot of nets to get through tonight. Not much is happening here, though. A few red salmon show up, a few dog salmon, and a king salmon here and there. Micah tells us his latest joke as we pick these salmon.

"Two men walked into a bar. They sat down. One said, 'Bring me some H_2O.' The other said, 'Bring me some H_2O too.' He drank it. Then he died."

Elisha and I look at each other blankly, then Elisha barks a laugh. "Yeah, I get it. H_2O_2. That's hydrogen peroxide, right?"

"Yep," Micah says, a bit chagrined. "How did you know?"

"Oh, just a little thing called chemistry."

I am loving this, being out here with my sons on the water, especially watching Elisha. Elisha is quick in the boat, his actions swift and smooth. Like all of my kids, he's been fishing regularly since he was six. They are out here on these nets three times a day, for anywhere from eight to fourteen hours a day. It's not glamorous. It's tedious and repetitive, the same work, the same nets over and over, day after day for the entire summer. I admire their endurance.

We finish the first net, go on to the second. By the time we're on the third net, and are now in the open Shelikof Strait, the swells from the previous storm are still rolling. And the wind has come up, from the northeast again. The sea is already stirred, and we are not talking. Micah and I are focused on the line work, on moving the gear down the skiff, on "popping" the sway buoys. The lines are all rigid-tight now, the skiff is carpeted in kelp, making every move slippery, and the skiff itself is pitching both side to side and front to back. Nothing happens now without careful intent and measurement. Where you step, how fast, grabbing the line, tossing the fish—the labor is immediately doubled in a chopping sea. We are finally done with this net, and the fun is long gone. My stomach is empty and beginning to roil. I am wishing I had eaten more at dinner.

The next net is off another island, a ten-minute pounding

ride away, as the seas increase. This isn't terrible weather, but we are taking on spray. When we land and begin the next net, the tops of some of the waves are curling over the stern. We cannot talk for the howl of the wind in our ears. It has only been three hours, but my arms are turning to rubber and my hands no longer want to grab. Elisha yells for me to catch the net. I try and cannot. Micah tries to help, but he is not much good in this weather. Of all my kids, he's the only one who struggles with motion sickness. It takes us three tries to get it.

I am working with gritted teeth now, willing my body to obey, to hold the lines tight, to pull on the sway buoy, but I am not doing well this night. I feel badly for Elisha, who is out in this blow with me instead of a young muscled crewman. My intent is to help, and I am not much help in this weather. I am not weak. I am not afraid of work or given to fear. I've always been strong for my size, strong compared to other women my age. But who am I fooling? I'll be fifty-seven in a few months. It's not fair to Elisha and Micah. It's clear I have to make a decision. I either have to get myself back in full strength—lifting weights—or decide that I'm done going out. That I will no longer fish at all. That will leave me shore bound, away from my kids much of the time. But it's time.

I feel a weight fall from my shoulders, but my decision doesn't help me now. I've still got several hours to go. I'd really like a rescue. And, being prone to prayer when I'm struggling, I cast some words above the wind, something like, *Please help me, Lord!* And I can't help glancing toward shore as well. Wouldn't this just be a lovely time for Jesus to show up? I mean the one with flesh and feet, who picked his way among the nets strung out along the beach of Galilee. I'd even settle for my pastor. If either one stood there, cupping hands and calling out, "Hey! Come on in!" I'd drop the green mesh from my sodden cotton gloves in a half-second. I'd turn sideways to squeeze past the totes that hold the fish. I'd nudge Elisha out of the stern, take over the outboard, explaining, "Hey, see that guy on the beach? He's calling me."

I can see Elisha blinking in disbelief even as the rain and spray drain down his face. "What are you doing? You can't just stop!" he would say, glancing to shore to see if anyone was really there. And of course, no one would be there. Jesus only did this once. Or twice. Two thousand years ago.

And of course fishermen don't ever stop in the middle of a net. Nor do you ever leave in the middle of a season. I've lived among the obsessiveness of fishermen for so many years, it almost makes me laugh to imagine the ruckus this would cause. Because fishermen—good fishermen, real fishermen—don't leave. They don't quit. Ever.

My friend and neighbor Dave Densmore has been working these same waters for fifty years. He started as a boy, fishing out in the Aleutians, running a seine boat at fifteen, the youngest I've ever heard of. He's sixty-nine now and hobbles on feet that were nearly amputated when he was adrift in a life raft for five winter days. He was close to freezing to death when his raft was discovered by a Japanese trawler. At the end of last season, Dave told me definitively, "This is it, my last one." I remember him saying that five years ago. He is back again this year, not even remembering he had threatened to retire.

Aaron, a fisherman I meet at the dock in Tiberias, Israel, will not leave his nets. He cannot make a living anymore fishing in the Sea of Galilee, but he does not stop. He supplements his income with a speedboat, pulling inner tubes for tourists during the tourist season. He's been fishing for forty years and will not stop.

And us. There have been summers when we worked unending hours every day of the week for four months—and earned nothing. Still, we came back the next year. It's a sickness. It's a disease. It's love. It's hope. Once you have spent any part of your life on water—living throbbing thrilling liquid moody dangerous unsinkable water—you cannot turn away. It gets inside you. No, it's already inside you. We are made of humus, it is true, of the soil itself, but the ocean roars in our chests, pulses through the river of our veins. And there, on the sea, blown about by winds, floating between sky and earth, working by tide and by fish instead of time, fishermen feel a kind of freedom from those who live on land, punching a daily clock. We are slaves to sea and fish, but somehow, paradoxically, we feel free. Why would we give this up?

But they did, those fishermen on the Sea of Galilee. Why did they do it? Why did they drop the nets as quickly as I'm tempted to do now? They have less excuse than me. It was not blowing or swelling; the men were not holding their bellies for fear of heaving. It was a calm day, a day like any other for them. Except for him. And did they know what he was asking of them? The Gospel account makes it all so simple, so immediate, and their obedience so unquestioning. "At once," it says, "they left their nets and followed him."[1] But they weren't just leaving the nets behind. They were leaving their family business. They were leaving their father. "At once." That fast.

I turn now and look at Elisha. His young beard is sparse, his eyes are half-lidded against the wind and spray as he shakes out finger kelp from the net. His face is neutral though I know he hates this—a whole carpet of kelp clings to the meshes and must be shaken out. We all hate it. I automatically help him, my own arms raising and lowering the net with him. Micah, beside me, follows suit. I am standing between them, my youngest son on my right, my middle son on my left. The three of us now, arms out, waving and vibrating the net in perfect unison. I glance at them and almost smile. I know they do not see this, the wonder of it.

And this is just what those men left behind. They left their father, and maybe even other brothers. And this business they had worked in together all their lives. How do you give this up? I have some idea what those years looked like, those years of training since they were small. First, where to sit in the boat, how to stay still and keep your place and not get in the men's way. Then how to pull on the net, where to pull, how to extract the fish, how to tie up to another boat and not get your fingers smashed between them. And among all this, all of us parents watching these little boys and my daughter making a way to play in the boat while the men work: the fish recruited as talking puppets, the bull kelp carved into flutes, the games and stories and falling asleep in the stern when the hour got late. And as they got older, Zebedee's sons learning cast-net fishing, learning how to throw the net, how to pull it back in neatly for the next throw—then fishing with trammel nets, another whole system to master. For Zebedee, the patient teaching on the oars, how to position them, how to dip them efficiently. For us, the gradual move to running the engine, the intricate steering and landing. Then teaching how to mend the nets. Then working in storms. Until the day the son or the daughter stands in the stern of their own boat—only fourteen, but on the water they're adults now, teaching their crewmen all they know, and driving out onto the ocean ahead of you or beside you. You still work together on the same nets, in the same ten miles of ocean, but now in separate boats. You still have to hire workers to help, but no hired men can replace your own sons and daughters.

I know how this feels, to be Zebedee, and to see your children called away from the nets. But for him, this is not the first time they have left. This is a second leaving. A much harder rivening, I am sure. As children, they would have left their father's boat to study in the synagogue school. Perhaps it was only mornings, but some part of each day was spent with all the other children ages five and up, studying the Torah, the first five books of the Bible, learning to read and write its words in Hebrew, memorizing as many of those words as possible. At age ten, most of the boys and girls returned home to work in their father's trade. Maybe they did as well, these sons of Zebedee. Or maybe they went on for just a few more years, from ten to thirteen, when they would have learned the Mishnah, the oral interpretations of the Torah.

I suspect these fishermen and brothers went back to the boats between ages thirteen and fifteen, when the exams were given for that next level, the highest level of study. Only the best and brightest made that cut. Perhaps one of the brothers could have made the cut, but their father needed them both. Successful fishing required several boats, big boats, and several men to work the nets. The trammel nets were complex, and required at least four to run them. I cannot know for sure, no one can, but I think it likely that those boys left synagogue study under pressure from their father. What business did they have becoming rabbis, if ever they should rise that high? They were fishermen! He could not operate without them.

Nor can we. My children are just the same. They leave fishing early to return to school—first elementary, then high school, then college. Duncan and the rest of the crew stay another month to finish the season. My kids leave for internships, to do research with a professor. And after college, what then? Will they leave fishing forever? I know how it feels, the empty place at the table, their skiff run by someone else. It's a loss. An aching loss. Will they come back? That's all we want to know, Zebedee and I.

We are nearing the hook of the net now. The waves have risen as we've moved further from shore. This net, the "Outside" we call it, is always hard no matter the weather. Riptides and currents cross and clash here on the edge of the Shelikof Strait. The wind keens one notch higher around my hooded face. I am breathing noisily through my mouth, stifling stomach cramps as the net passes through Micah's hands, then mine. I see a rogue wave coming, one nearly twice the size of the others. The skiff rises, and we rise with it, the net in our hands tautening like a string of steel. At the top of the wave, I crane my head toward Seven-mile Beach. Are they there yet? Are they coming? By the time we get to this net, the others are usually on their way.

Jesus isn't likely to show up in body, but the other skiffs will at some point. That will be a good enough rescue tonight. And there—I see it! The distant snout of a skiff, pointing through the horizon's waves. Coming toward us. The night will soon be done. I feel better already. Four skiffs are down there, about five miles away from where we are now. All the skiffs go out at the same time, coordinated in an orderly scatter, each to their assigned disparate nets, as far apart as ten miles. Those fishermen—my other sons and their crewmen—will work their way net to net toward us, just as we are working island to island, net to net toward them, until all skiffs converge on the last net, each skiff nestling in beside the other, sometimes bumping with a metallic clunk as we finish together. It's a massive ballet, performed three times a day, all of us swinging slowly toward each other, mile by mile, until we see one another's eyes and hands again: Jeff from Missouri, Brian from Kentucky, Tucker from South Dakota, Sean from Idaho, the brothers from Georgia. College graduates, construction workers, seminary students, a rancher, a Bible school graduate headed for the mission field, a college chemistry major, a musician, and my sons . . . all draped in the same neon orange, launched and swelling on the same waters, rising and falling together.

They would have known that too, those brothers working with their father and crew, like us, a family band in boats. Like us, they would not have spoken this, how well they knew the geometry and poetry of it all. But they dropped their nets and tossed them in their storage box, with maybe something of a flutter of joy in their stomachs. Why? I can only guess.

I can see it all. I walked most of that shoreline around Galilee, beating my way through the reeds, lost among a trail of boulders one morning, feet sinking in the mud near Yardenit. I walked the gravelly beach where it might have happened. For some reason, Jesus turned away from the synagogue that day, where the best students and teachers hung out. He turned from the halls of learning and religiosity to the beach. To them, the laborers who followed in their fathers' footsteps, the ones who hadn't made the cut. The dropouts. They had to marvel at this—that the one John called "the lamb of God" was pursuing *them*, was choosing *them*! The famous rabbis just a generation before them, Hillel and Shammai, didn't usually work like that. It was the brightest students who chose the rabbi, the master they wanted to follow and pattern their lives after. But this rabbi was choosing *them*—*and* was choosing them *first*! Not last, not in a last-ditch effort to round out his crew, to fill some kind of quota. And likely not because he could find no other willing volunteers. No one else was standing beside him as he called, *Come, follow after me!*

So. They chose him back. They had to. Everything about him invited them closer, nearer. How could they turn away from this? They didn't know yet what they were being called to be or to do, but they said yes. They understood, as everyone did, that "follow" meant literally "to walk the same road." They understood they were being called into a relationship with this man, a teacher-student relationship. They said yes to that. They said yes to *him*. With a lift of their arms, they gave one final toss to their net, in the storage box with their other gear. They retrieved their robes, and I see them there, now three, walking the beach. The brothers are not sure what they've done. It scares them, and it excites them too.

Just three months after that pick with my boys I am sitting in a church in Tiberias, on the shore of Galilee. It is my last day there. I am walking the promenade when I hear faint singing and realize with a start it is Sunday. I follow the voices tentatively into a small stone church. About twenty people stand singing in a narrow sanctuary above wooden pews. Three priests stand officiously before them, and two young women, one with a flute, the other with a guitar, play beside them. I creep in, shrink into a pew near the back. I look overhead—there he is, front and center in faded mosaics, sitting in the stern of a boat, hands on a tiller, sail billowing overhead. No nets, no fish, just Peter sailing effortlessly in his boat. We pray the Our Father, recite the Apostles' Creed, take Communion by intinction, all under Peter, no longer a fisherman.

After the service, I approach the priest, a white-haired man with the smooth skin of a boy. "Why do you think Jesus chose so many fishermen?"

He thinks for just a moment. "Because they were used to depending entirely upon the providence of God. Not like farmers, who can calculate everything. But fishermen cannot control the sea. They never know if they will catch a lot, or anything. Fishermen must depend on God, as we do. They already knew how to do this."

I nod encouragingly, writing his words down in a notebook.

"It's all an analogy," he goes on, gesturing to the mosaic on the dome and the nautical scenes on the walls. "The boat is like the church. We are the nets, the instruments of God. But we never know what we will catch."

I thank him for his time as he hurriedly turns to his next responsibility. But I am disappointed at his second response. Analogy and allegory is just too simple. Do water, boats, a net, fish gain some higher spiritual value by what they represent rather than what they are? I think God means something through their simple material existence. But we have done this throughout history, peering beyond the created world—what

God has made and what we have made of it—into a hoped-for higher meaning. And some of it started right here, this moment when Jesus calls these fishermen *away* from their nets, from fishing for fish to now fish for human souls instead.

I want to protest, of course—me, the woman whose family still keeps daily hands on real-fleshed fish. Does following Jesus mean we must all leave the material world of commerce behind in the quest for souls? And does this mean that all of us who have not chosen the clergy have chosen the lesser of the two— the world of the flesh over the world of the spirit? Why aren't we all out fishing for men and women with the net of the gospel?

Standing there in that sanctuary, I can hear the wind whirring around the dome and the rising waves pounding the stone jetty. Passersby will be splashed by the whooshing waves overhead. This Galilee water is as wet now as it was then. I realize suddenly that Jesus did indeed take them from the nets that day, but he did not take them from the water, nor did he take them entirely from the boats, either. After that call, there would be boats and sea crossings and storms still to come. And nothing was better than teaching from a boat. Nor did he take them entirely from the fish because fish were everywhere in that world, one of the staple foods of the whole area, and you could not feed a multitude on a hillside without a few fish. Nor could you pay taxes without catching a fish that might be harboring a coin in its mouth. Nor could you show your friends the physicality of your risen body without picking up some fish and roasting them over a fire on the beach to share with your astounded grieving friends, who thought you so dead . . .

I can take a breath. When Jesus called them from the fish to become fishers of men, he was not done with any of this yet. I'm still here in this world of matter, of flesh and water, of making a living—a world that we all recognize, that we all still live and move and have our being in. I'm not leaving yet. Following him does not mean abandoning this world. Jesus was a *man*, after all. Fully man, as feet-in-the-mud as the rest of us.

I am making a decision as well. I cannot imagine what would have happened if those fishermen had not left their nets, had not walked the gospel out into the villages and cities, bringing good news to all who were dying. But I want to stay out here. Even this night, thrown by wind and wave, I'm not ready to cave. I'm not ready to give in—to the water, to the weather, to my age. I've been on and around these very waters for almost four decades. I believed God called me here to this island, to this water. There's more for me to do here. There's more for me to understand here. I don't want to leave it—ever. I don't want to forget how it feels to pull a salmon from the deep green ocean, cradling its heft in my arms. I can't go out daily, as my husband and kids do, but I will go out as I can. I'm not ready to give it up. Maybe when I'm seventy, but not now.

Those fishermen left their nets to follow God. I will follow him by staying.

CHAPTER FOUR

THE CATCH OF CATCHES

One day as Jesus was standing by the Lake of Gennesaret, the people were crowding around him and listening to the word of God. He saw at the water's edge two boats, left there by the fishermen, who were washing their nets. He got into one of the boats, the one belonging to Simon, and asked him to put out a little from shore. Then he sat down and taught the people from the boat.

When he had finished speaking, he said to Simon, "Put out into deep water, and let down the nets for a catch."

Simon answered, "Master, we've worked hard all night and haven't caught anything. But because you say so, I will let down the nets."

When they had done so, they caught such a large number of fish that their nets began to break. So they signaled their partners in the other boat to come and help them, and they came and filled both boats so full that they began to sink.

When Simon Peter saw this, he fell at Jesus' knees and said, "Go away from me, Lord; I am a sinful man!" For he and all his companions were astonished at the catch of fish they had taken, and so were James and John, the sons of Zebedee, Simon's partners.

Then Jesus said to Simon, "Don't be afraid; from now on you will fish for people." So they pulled their boats up on shore, left everything and followed him.

LUKE 5:1-11

I AM WALKING THE PROMENADE in Tiberias early this morning, hoping to catch sight of fishermen heading out to their nets. It's windy, the first wind I've seen here. The waters are chopping into flecks of white. The boardwalk is empty, except for a father and a son flying a kite. The restaurants that line the promenade are set with crisp linens, ready for a dinner crowd tonight. I scan the main dock, which harbors three of the Holy Land boats and a handful of smaller dinghies and sport boats, all that're left in the water for the winter season. I am about to give up, disappointed, when I see a man sitting on the steps in boots. Knee boots. The kind fishermen might wear. I take a deep breath and near the dock gate. He is facing away from me.

"Excuse me, do you speak English?" I venture.

He turns to look at me. "Yah, a leetle." He is completely bald, with a brown face and heavy black eyebrows. He looks at me with curiosity.

"Are you a fisherman?"

"Yah, I'm a fisherman." He nods.

"Me, too," I said. "I'm from Alaska. We fish for salmon. Do you know salmon?"

"Alaska! Salmone!" He gets up from his step and faces me, the dock gate between us. "Yes, I see on TV documentary. Big fish!" And he opens his arms about two feet.

"Yes!" I nod back, laughing.

"You? Fisherman?" He is puzzled.

"Yes, sometimes. And all of my family—all fishermen. Look, I have some video. I show you!" I did not plan this, but I remember that I have two videos from fishing still on my iPhone.

He opens the gate from inside and steps out onto the concrete boardwalk, standing just a foot away from me. I pull out the phone, find the videos, and play the first one. We are on the ocean traveling in a skiff. Suddenly an enormous fin whale surfaces just a few feet from our skiff, blasting air and sea through its cavernous blowhole.

"Whoa! What fish . . . ahhhhh . . ." He searches for the word.

"Whale. It's a fin whale."

"Fin whale," he repeats.

"Here, let me play it again."

The fisherman laughs this time, shaking his head. I am guessing he is about my age, or a bit older.

"Here's another one." I play the next, video shot out in a big storm blowing at least thirty miles per hour, the water peeled to white, the skiffs pitching madly, the nets straining, all the fishermen encased in orange rain gear, hoods over faces, like wraiths. This one too is short, just fifteen seconds.

"Oohhhh, big storm," he says and whistles under his breath. A man starts to pass us while we are watching. The fisherman calls to him in Hebrew. He comes over to watch with us. I play it again.

When it is over, the fisherman speaks to the other in Hebrew, but I hear "Alaska" and "salmone" while they both look at me with interest.

I hope I've established my credentials. "What do you fish for here?"

"Everything. I fish everything here: musht, biny, carp." He waves his hand.

"Where is your boat?"

"There." He points to a small wooden dinghy painted blue

at the end of the short dock. I see his net in the boat, a clear monofilament made in Japan. This would pass no kind of muster in Alaska, either the net or the boat, but I try not to judge or be disappointed by anything.

"When do you go out?" I hope I'm not being too pushy, but I'll be leaving Israel soon.

"At night. In the morning." He is noncommittal. "Now it's too windy. Too much waves. I'm waiting if the wind comes down," he says, looking out at the water.

I follow his eyes, trying to see what he sees. I guess the wind to be close to twenty miles per hour, what we would call a day breeze, but the water has only a small chop. In Alaska, we wouldn't give it a second thought. But then I see his boat. It is toy-sized, just fifteen feet, and the sides look no more than two feet high.

We talk for thirty more minutes. He tells me his name—Aaron—and his story. He's been fishing on the lake since he was fifteen. Forty other small boats work the waters, supporting about a hundred people, he tells me. And there is only one bigger boat, a seine boat that's still allowed to fish. There used to be three seine boats, but they fished too well. They caught too many fish. Now there are not so many fish as there used to be, he tells me. I listen to all this with both sadness and fascination. It's the same story around the world—greed and overfishing. I ask more and more questions. But what I really need is some kind of commitment.

"When the wind comes down and you go out, I can go out with you?" I ask one more time. I lift my voice so I am not too assertive. Though, in Israel, I've observed that assertiveness is valued more than politeness.

"Yah, yah!" He waves his head and hand impatiently like we've gone over this a hundred times.

It's nearly 5:00 p.m. Dark now. This is a definite downside of coming in November. There's twice as much daylight as back home, but the days end too soon for all I want to do. I step into the boat cautiously, feeling like I'm going to tip it over. It's so small, and the sides come up just to my knees. Is there really room for me? In our skiffs back home, the sides come up to my hips, high enough to allow all kinds of out-of-boat leanings over the water. Aaron takes his place in the stern, beside the fifteen-horse outboard, and Ben, his crewman, sits near him. I sit in the bow. Aaron pulls the engine to life, and we rumble out of the tiny harbor in the dark.

The wind blows for two more days after I meet this Galilean fisherman. Every morning and evening, I walk from my hotel down to his dock to see if he is there. I find him two more times. Each time we talk some more, lamenting over the wind and waves, and set another time to meet. Finally we are motoring out of the tiny harbor. I feel a quiet moment of victory as we glide out onto the black water, away from the lights of the harbor. Three days of waiting, checking, and wrangling to get here.

Aaron seems happy enough that I am here, but Ben is not. He glowers at me silently. He's twenty-eight, single, and because I don't speak Hebrew and he doesn't speak English, we cannot communicate. As soon as we are out of the harbor, Ben pulls out a package of chocolate cookies and cigarettes. They both start in on the chocolate and light up between cookies. Aaron has clearly eaten a lot of cookies out here. Ben silently offers me the cookies in the dark. I smile and take two and know this is one reason Aaron won't give up fishing. There are certain permissions that come to you on the water that you don't possess on land. Doctor's orders, health concerns, wife's orders—none of that matters on the water. I know how it is, the distinct economies of water life and land life. I don't eat candy bars at home on land, but I'll eat one in the skiff. There's work to be done, and that's all that matters.

My expectations are high, but Aaron is low-key. It's near the end of the musht season, he tells me. I know from my reading that musht is the Hebrew name for tilapia. The lake levels are low, but the price is good right now. He sells mostly to the restaurants on the promenade. The tourist season is dying as Christmas nears, but still, nearly every tourist who comes to the Sea of Galilee will have a dinner of this St. Peter's fish.

While we eat and chug along, I am so excited to finally be out on this lake with a fisherman, I cannot stop smiling. Aaron laughs at me and says, "Look at you! So happy! You like fishing, no?" I laugh and nod. Yes, this makes me happy, but I am here for more than this, of course. I have not tried to explain to him the fuller reason I am here, my own search. I do not tell him that I cannot know this place without being on its waters. I do not tell him that I am here to find the real gospel. And how do I explain that I am here on this lake to find Jesus in my own waters back home? I can hardly explain it to myself.

When they get to where they'll set the net, they stand and pull out a box of rain gear. Ben steps into a pair of rain pants that are far too big for him. He struggles with the straps, which are too loose. He snaps them into place, finally, and begins helping Aaron put out the net. As he leans over to put the net out, his straps keep slipping over his shoulders. Reflexively he fixes them again and again, with growing annoyance. Should I help? Finally, when the two are still for a moment, I touch Ben's shoulder. He turns around as if I've slugged him. We stand just inches apart. I hold up my finger. "Wait." I unsnap his straps, and crisscross them over his back so some of the slack is taken, and they won't slip. It takes just a few seconds. I know he is embarrassed to be helped by this motherly American woman, but both our lives will be easier now. Aaron looks at me and nods. Ben shrugs his shoulders, now with straps that fit, he nods, and we are off again.

We are out for several hours—setting the nets, detergent bottles for buoys. The nets are much smaller than ours, and the mesh openings are smaller too. They are lighter, just mono-filament, where ours are multi-strand, heavier for heavier fish, for strong tides and hard weather. I want to help, but Aaron is teaching Ben, and there is no room for me to stand, nor is there anything I can do. It's a simple process. Aaron drives the boat slowly parallel to the shore, watching his little sonar screen. When he thinks there are fish, he shifts into neutral. We drift while he and Ben spool out the net behind them. We set one net. While the net is not deep—only three meters, and it sinks a meter below the surface—it is long, five hundred meters long.

We go on to another part of the lake to set the second net and to let the first net soak. I am surprised that they stay so close to shore. We are never more than a hundred feet from shore. I am surprised that fishermen on the Sea still fish in the dark, as Peter, Andrew, and the others did. The reason is the same—so the fish don't see the nets, and some fish are attracted to the light.

I have one more surprise coming. After setting both long nets, letting them soak, pulling them in, in all that expanse, through all that water, two tiny fish appear, neither sellable. We fish half the night—and catch nothing.

This happens to us, too, in Alaska, of course. I write this in the midst of our own blank season here on our sea, the end of June, the weeks between the early red salmon run in June and the pink salmon run in July. For two to three weeks every year, my family will come in, peeling off their wet, salty clothes to hang them by the oil stove. I will ask, "How did it go?" And in these days they will say, "We got five fish off the Harvester nets." "We did four nets and picked seven fish." "We didn't even have enough to deliver." Or even, "We picked five nets and caught nothing. Not one." At mealtime, my sons or Peter or Josh, our crewmen this year, will pray, "Lord, bless us with fish."

It's the blank season, when we catch trees, grass, kelp, jellyfish—everything but fish. One night Abraham came in and reported he had caught a stereo speaker in the net. The summer after the tsunami, we caught a five-foot plastic buoy from Japan. One year we found some Nike sneakers tangled in the web: A freighter carrying vans of the famous shoes lost a few containers overboard, littering our beaches. Even without fish, we still must work: We still run the nets through our skiff and our hands, tending and caring for them, doing all that we can to invite the fish, to make the net fish-worthy should a single one or a school swim by. The fishing season is short enough without these lost days. We have so many bills to pay to even be out here. The fuel and food costs alone are enormous. We know we're working hard—for nothing. But after more than fifty years out here, we've come to expect these frustrating weeks.

Maybe, on one of these net-empty days, something happens. What if it went like this?

We have been fishing all day long, out on the nets hour after hour, keeping them clean, but they are empty. No fish. All day.

We finally come in at the end of the day, discouraged, and the man we saw the other day—he's a minister of some sort, we think—meets us here on our beach. We're a little surprised to see him. This is our beach, our working space. He's not a fisherman. He doesn't really belong here. But there he is, smiling and friendly. We're always glad to see a friendly face. But then he says something surprising:

"Hey, Duncan and Leslie! Good to see you! Look, I know you want fish. Go on back out and put out another net right here in the channel."

We look at him to see if he's joking. He looks back, still smiling, his eyes direct and clear. It's a ridiculous idea. We're tired. It's not dark, of course, because this is summer in Alaska, but the day is long over. Our nets are established right where they are. We don't just move them. And we tell him so: "Listen, we've been out fishing for days. We haven't caught a thing. And we know why. It's not a mystery. The red run is over and the pink run hasn't yet begun. This happens every year. The pink salmon just aren't running yet."

We explain it all patiently. After all, this man is not a fisherman. He works on shore. From what we've seen, most of his work is talking, teaching. Clearly he knows about spiritual things, but what can he know about real things, about nature, about the cycles of salmon? Every man has his area. This isn't his. Otherwise he wouldn't send us back out. And—he wouldn't send us out into the channel. There are never any fish in the channel. We tried, stringing a net out there for years. But no longer. Every summer we watch seine boats come and try their luck in the channel. They try for half a day maybe, while we watch and smile. They always give up and leave.

So, yes, rookie mistake, to think there are salmon in the channel. But—we've heard him speak. He has a kind of wisdom we've not heard before. We're not entirely sure who he is. We know there's something else about him that we can't name, but it's compelling. We're intrigued and want to know more from him.

"Okay," we answer with an inward sigh. We're not given to compliance, especially when it comes to our work. That's why we're out here in the first place instead of in a nine-to-five job. But we also know the best way to teach someone something is to demonstrate it, let its results speak for itself. We'll soon show him that it's best for each man to keep to his own expertise.

We pick up an extra net stored in the warehouse, step back wearily into our skiff, push off from the beach, and head back out on the water, straight out into the channel. We hope our neighbors aren't watching. We hope no other boats will come by as we put out the net. We'll be so humiliated.

We let out the net and go straight out into the channel. It takes ten minutes to set it out. As soon as we drop the anchor, we go back to the first part of the net ready to pull it up and bring it all back in. All this extra work for nothing, just to prove a point. Just to establish, at least, our willingness to humor this man. After all, that's probably what this is about, we realize, Duncan and I, as we work the net. We're satisfied with our response and hope he is as well. As we slow the skiff to pick up the net and pull it in, we freeze.

We see silver beneath us, nothing but flashing silver. We cannot even see the net, it is so full. The net is full. Full, as in, every mesh of the net holds a salmon. It's a throng of salmon, at least a thousand of them, filling every single mesh! The net, in fact, has sunk. The corks can't hold such weight, and the whole mess is so heavy it's three feet underwater.

Our hearts explode. We turn to one another, scream in excitement, call to shore, "Noah! Naphtali! Boys! Bring a skiff!"

And they come running, no matter how tired they are. They're not quite believing us yet, but they hear the urgency in our voices and push the skiff in, fire the outboard, zoom out into the channel—the channel? They come alongside, see the sunken net, and together we all lean into the water, pulling the net up as we can, picking the fish out one by one from the water, our own arms underwater. We know how to do this. There have been seasons before when the nets were so filled and so heavy we could not lift them into the boat, and instead, we leaned out into the water. But not in the channel. And never this time of year.

Our arms are flashing now as silver flies from the water to the skiffs, until the boats are so heavy, we have only a few inches of freeboard. No one is talking. This is a fishing emergency, and it requires every inch of effort. We can't help but do some mental calculations as we pick the fish, though. The price is decent this year, so each fish is worth about six dollars. If we get a thousand fish, we're looking at six thousand dollars right here, right now. I think of paying my sons' school costs. Duncan is thinking of paying ahead on our mortgage. These fish will solve so many problems for us! Our arms are pumping, and the fish are flying.

We've forgotten that we're tired. We've forgotten where we are. We've forgotten why we're there. It seems we'll never get all the fish from the net. But I glance over at my son and daughter's boat, and I see they are filling as fast we are. Two thousand fish, then! Twelve thousand dollars! Maybe we can finally go on that trip! Maybe Naphtali can pay her grad school bills! As soon as we pick one from a mesh, another fills its place, until suddenly I realize I'm not leaning out of the boat, the freeboard is gone: I'm leaning in the water. Both skiffs are tipped too far, taking on water.

"Stop!" Duncan screams. "Stop picking fish and start bailing!" We realize we're going to lose all the fish if we can't stay afloat. What good are these fish if we can't secure them? We've got to be able to move them to the tender, the delivery boat. We get up from our posts on the edge of the skiff, leaving the fish still in the net, and look for a bailer. I grab the five-gallon bucket and start filling and dumping, Duncan finds another bucket, Naphtali and Noah in the other skiff do the same, frantically—all our fish are at risk now.

In ten minutes, we are safe again. Both skiffs are more loaded than I've ever seen, with more salmon than I've ever seen in a skiff. We don't have totes—we didn't expect to catch a single fish, so we are standing in fish up to our thighs, just like the old days. We stand up straight, for the first time in three hours, twisting and cracking our backs back into place. We look at each other and sigh with exhaustion and joy, too. These fish are just what we need!

Suddenly we see him, the minister, sitting up in the bow. He's been here with us all along, but we've been so frantic we forgot about him. He's standing in just as many fish as we are. Did he help us? We don't remember, but suddenly we remember why we're here. All four of us are staring at this man, then the fish, then around us at the channel, then the man's face, who hasn't taken his eyes off us. We are terrified.

It's not hard to see this scene almost two thousand years ago.

I see Simon looking at Jesus at that same moment. His eyes are wide and flat. How does this man know? About the fish. About me. About this very moment. To sink the boats—yes! Once they had a catch that nearly sank their boat. They talked about that for years! And just once more, he wanted to be that lucky, that good of a fisherman. They'd talk about him—Simon the Great Fisherman—all along the shore of Galilee for years to come. He'd build on to his house. He'd be someone people knew about. Maybe he'd get a better seat in the synagogue. That's all he wanted—just one boatload of fish! And it wasn't just about him. It was about his family, too. He wanted that money for his wife, for his children.

Is it possible that this man knows his greatest secret, that his deepest disappointment was leaving synagogue school? He went with all the other children in his early years, learning to read and write Hebrew so he could learn the Torah, the first five books of Moses. They were "people of the Book," these Jews, and especially those who lived in Galilee, tucked away in the north hill country, away from the pagan influences of Jerusalem. Everyone knew that their work as the chosen people of God was to "be holy as I am holy," words they had memorized from Leviticus. He had been devoted to his studies of the Torah, but he was a fisherman's son first and always. He couldn't stay in school. He was a competitive sort, though—always the first to speak, to leap, to jump in and get the work done better than anyone else. If he couldn't be the best student of the Torah, he would be the best fisherman!

This man, this rabbi, whoever he was, watched him closely. Simon's mouth fell open. The boatload of fish. His heart was so tight he knew it would split, like the nets. He stepped toward Jesus and fell, his body now in the mass of thrashing fish. He wanted to grab Jesus' knees, right in front of him, but he was afraid to touch him.

"You must go!" He is crying. He's fallen in more fish than he's ever caught, and he hates these fish now. This man, this man who Simon wanted to show up as a rookie. Who was he, then? How did he see that school of musht there when nobody else did? Simon knew himself as a master fisherman. He knew this lake, the way the fish moved during the various seasons. Can it be possible that *this* man is master over these elements instead of him? Or—maybe he sent the fish? That couldn't be possible. And then, he has a worse thought: Surely he didn't *create* those fish? Simon's gut goes tight and he suddenly sees into his own shrunken heart—and he loathes himself. He knows he deserves to die. He *will* die if this man with piercing eyes stays here, so close to him! "Go, leave me, Lord! I'm full of sin! Please, go!"[1] Everything Simon thought he know about fishing and about himself—is wrong. Completely, upside-down wrong. Who is this man?

The darkness of his own heart overwhelms him. The truest words he knows spill out: "I'm a sinful man!" Simon *must* send Jesus away. He is too unworthy for his attention, for even his presence. But Peter does not know that these terrified words of confession are exactly what will qualify him to be a disciple. He doesn't have to be a brilliant student of the Torah. He doesn't have to be a successful fisherman. In fact, his work that night was utterly futile. He only needs to know his need.

And Jesus doesn't answer what we think. He doesn't say, "Oh no, Simon, you're fine! You're not as bad as all that." He doesn't deny what the fisherman has just seen of himself. But he's not here standing in fish to condemn anyone, no matter how accurate their revelation. "Don't be afraid,"[2] he speaks gently.

And in those words—"Fear not!"—we hear it. We remember all the times in Scripture some brilliant being, angel or man, appears before a man or a woman, and is so dazzling with purity and goodness, all fall down. No one can stand or live in its presence. No one wants to die, and how else to live but to send away this being, this angel—and now, this Yeshua, who is too far, too good to come near. Let us live our own tiny dark lives—it's all we know. It's safe. Go away! You are too much for us! We cannot abide this abundance!

"Don't be afraid." And surely Jesus means, *Don't be afraid of yourself. Don't be afraid of me.*

And then the next words that don't seem to fit: "From now on, you'll catch people instead of fish."[3]

He's not asking. He's not inviting. It's more forceful than the words in Matthew and Mark's story, where this man on the beach invites them appealingly, "Come, follow after me." And there's a promise with that one: "And if you do, here is what I will do with you and for you. I will enable you to fish for men." This call is stronger, more directive. Are these callings the same, seen and heard differently by different writers and witnesses? Or did both of these happen on the same day? Or on different days? I do not know. Scholars and commentators are divided.

But these words—can we hear how strange they were to these men? "From now on you will catch people instead of fish." This wasn't normal rabbi talk. The image of throwing out a net and catching people had to be unsettling, even ludicrous.

Where does it say that in the Torah? But what was normal about any of this? A rabbi choosing his students out in a boat, when everyone is covered in fish gurry, instead of in the synagogue, bent over the words of God? Those four fishermen couldn't have known what he meant, but right here, right from the start, Jesus was signaling something new. Something different. This was not a rabbi's usual pitch or promise to his potential students and followers. Followers were the sharpest students of God's laws and the Mishnah and Midrash, their traditions and interpretations of that law. Signing on to follow a rabbi meant becoming a more knowledgeable student. It meant they could better argue the fine points of God's Word. But this man, this Teacher, is promising something else. He says, "You *will* catch people." He's promising action, not just words and knowledge. And he's promising that they will be a part of this action, whatever it is, not simply observers.

The whole day is confusing—and compelling. Something happens within each man's heart, each man dripping with sweat and lake water, their fishing clothes dirty with their work, musht scales flecking their bare arms and legs. Maybe one of them sees—if this man can fill their nets with fish, if he can transform failure into unthinkable bounty, what might he do with us, this boatload of fishermen? They look at one another, these men who have worked together most of their young lives. They speak a few words in low voices, and look again at Jesus. They row their fish-heavy boats to shore, they land in the crowd of watchers shouting and exclaiming over their haul. They unload the musht right there to the venders, collecting their wages, more than they've earned in a month of fishing. They coil their nets, put their shoulders to the boats, and push them above the high-water mark, and they leave together, five of them, the crowd behind them calling after them.

If we somehow missed it in Matthew and Mark, Luke is going to make it harder for us, this whole calling and following business. We know the Kingdom of God scene doesn't get started until Jesus casts his own net and hauls in some men. We know the story so well; it feels inevitable that they should dump their nets and go. But I tell you again: This is not what fishermen do. Especially not when fishermen haul in the catch of their lives, which means money in the hand. For some fishermen in some fisheries, it can mean tens, even hundreds of thousands of dollars. A single haul of mackerel in the North Sea will net more than two million dollars. No one walks away from this. They do the opposite. When my family has a good season, we invest more money in our equipment, we might buy another skiff, we might hire another crewman. We plant ourselves further and deeper. If it happened once, no matter how miraculous, it will happen again. At every fish camp, no matter how poor the season before, we always believe the next will be better. Fishermen live on long shots and hope.

I cannot help but wonder, *Why did Jesus do it this way?* Why give them the catch of their lives—and then call them away from it? Why not call them right then, after they fished all night and caught nothing, when they most realize the emptiness of it, the gamble they take every time they drop a net into the water? How little control they have over what comes, or doesn't. Why not then? Isn't that enough—to say, "Look, that's what fishing is about; can you see it for what it is now? You can work all night long and come up with nothing. Now, come with me, and things will be different. No more gambling, no more uncertainty. You'll haul in a big catch for sure!"

But he didn't do this or say this. He gave them what they always wanted, what they talked about, hoped for, longed for, dreamed about—nets splitting with fish, crowds gaping, stacks of coins clinking in their hands. He made their wildest, fishiest dreams come true. And then asked them to leave it. Is this unreasonable, cruel? I see this as grace. Huge, billowing grace, as full as those nets. They knew what they were leaving, then. They had seen it, the most and best that could happen. They felt it, the thrill, the excitement, the money. There's nothing more after that. It never gets better. That's all there is. Enjoy it. Count the fish. Now, come. I have something far greater for you.

I have been there in those fish a hundred times over. There's death that comes in surfeit, affliction that comes in abundance. My first years fishing, five of us ran eight nets. We dropped with exhaustion every night, plowed under with fish. Then the years we call "Humpy Hell," in 2005 and 2006. The smothering of abundance, when you get what you hope for—nets sunk with fish, boats sinking with fish, and you are slain. You can hardly stand for the work. You cannot sleep with the swelling of the hands. And you know, in the middle of all of it, no matter how much you need that money, you know—it's not enough. The money wasn't enough. That year, the price of pink salmon fell to five cents a pound. A skiff-load of fish that broke your back to pick fetched a few hundred dollars. Whatever the paycheck was, all the expenses had to be paid, and your share of what was left was less than ten percent, there were so many others to split the check with. There were a few years when the money was good. But money, a lot or a little, won't resurrect you. It won't lift your head over your breakfast. It won't give your children back their playtime, their innocence. Money won't patch up your marriage when you can hardly speak to each other. You are slain, emptied of everything except the desire to sleep. And the fish, vacant and innocent, keep coming. And then you know: What you thought you wanted more than anything—can kill you.

Something died that day, I believe, that day of the miracle on the sea. Some dreams were fulfilled, then finished, freeing them to leave. Freeing them to pursue a deeper desire that maybe even they could not name themselves.

They left the nets. But I am not entirely done protesting. I have one complaint left. Did they really leave "everything"? Surely that's an exaggeration for our benefit—for all who come after. Look at them, the first disciples! They obeyed instantly, they dropped everything for him! This is our model. Haven't I heard this in college, in mission conferences, the disciples trotted out before us, their instant obedience. The speaker, the president of a missions organization, crying and trying to call us down the aisle to give our lives to missions, to go overseas, to Africa, anywhere Jesus calls! To drop whatever major we were considering, to dump our nets, our boats, and give it all up to be "fishers of men." This passage, this moment, weighs like a burden and cuts like a weapon against all of us with plans and regular jobs, all of us with children and parents and family businesses.

Did those first disciples really leave *everything*?

There's another passage that answers this. Jesus is talking to his closest friends, all of them now, and he tells them something depressing, something astounding. A man with lots of money wants salvation. He's done everything right. Jesus asks him just one thing more: to sell all he has and give it to the poor. The man's face falls. He can't do it. He can't give up his security, his life.

How hard it is for the rich to enter the kingdom of God! Jesus comments as the man walks away sad.

The twelve sitting there, who have just watched this happen, don't want to hear this. The rich give money to the temple. They support the synagogue. Everyone knows the rich can pave their way to heaven on their own dime. They hold the power, the best places in the synagogue. It's always been that way. There's security in this system.

"If even the rich can't get in, then who can be saved?" the men ask, shaken.[4]

Jesus looks at them, knowing how scared they are right now, and says, "With man this is impossible, but not with God; all things are possible with God."

And now comes Simon Peter, who can hardly stand this whole conversation. He's listening, his heart pounding, his hands clenching. He bursts: "We have left *everything* to follow You!"[5] And I know what else he says and thinks: *And still this isn't enough? If the rich can't get to heaven, what hope do we have, we who now have nothing! We used to have something, Jesus, remember? We gave it all up for you! Please tell us this counts for something!*

Jesus looks at him with love, and says, "Truly I tell you . . . no one who has left home or brothers or sisters or mother or father or children or fields for me and the gospel will fail to receive a hundred times as much in this present age . . . and in the age to come eternal life."[6]

It is *enough*, Jesus says. *Whatever you lose for my sake, you'll get it back—more, more than you can imagine.*

They did, then, leave it all. "Everything" is not hyperbole. But it's likely that they did not leave everything all at once. The leaving came in stages, from shorter times with Jesus to trips and then longer journeys by his side until they had indeed given up everything: parents, siblings, wives—even, I think, children. Yes, I think children. And they themselves were children leaving their parents.

Some might name this irresistible grace, that when Jesus calls, we have no choice but to respond. But they had a choice, and they chose to leave. It's not what fishermen do. But in that moment of choosing, they are not fishermen. They are men of Israel, sons of Abraham, Isaac, and Jacob, longing to see the coming of the One promised. And, they are told, this might be him.

I will let them go, then, these fishermen, away from their nets. The call came to them. They had to go.

When I stop reading this account through the eyes of a mother, worrying about my own children leaving, I remember—I left too. I left my mother, my father, my siblings, my town, my waitress-ing work—all that I knew, I left behind. I was called not *away* from the fishing nets—but *to* the fishing nets five thousand miles away from my home and family. Was it Jesus who called—or my husband? Or both? Did I go out of fear or faith? I am not sure. But I do know this: I left everything to come to this new life. I did not know fully what was before me. I thought I knew, but I didn't. I only knew I could not stay behind.

I don't believe it was easy for these men to leave their nets and lives. Nor has it been easy for anyone who has left "every-thing" because somehow God showed up, in body or in voice. It has not been easy for me, either. I am still paying the price of that leaving four decades ago. I first heard the call of Jesus as a young teenager, barely thirteen. I was quietly thrilled to be a teen, especially the day in December when I was invited to a youth group sledding party. My older sister's friend invited us, the one I knew was a little weird and "churchy." I had so few friends in this tiny New Hampshire village, I was excited to go. And scared. I had no idea what a "youth group" was, and the event was two towns over, so I wouldn't know most of the kids. But social events were rare.

I don't remember much of the sledding, but I remember what happened afterward. The twenty of us fell noisily into the basement of a little white country church beside the road, behind the man who was the leader of the group. He was in his twenties, I would guess, with auburn hair and an unremarkable face, but he was kind and good at throwing snowballs. He stood up front while we settled into chairs. I had no feeling of dread or anticipation for what would come. I didn't know it was a typical tactic, to invite non-Christian friends to a party, then hit them with the gospel. And if I had known, I would have come anyway.

He began to speak in a casual voice, telling us about God, who he was, what he asked of us. He read from the Bible. I don't remember the verses, but I do know I stopped breathing. Nor could I move for fear of missing a word. He was naming everything I wanted—to know God. To find him. To be known by him. To love him. To speak to him whenever I wanted. I couldn't do this. I had tried to pray for years, pitching desperate words skyward, past the ceiling of my room, words aimed to a throne somewhere up there, to a god I knew was there but didn't know. I did know some stories. I went to a Congregational church part of my sixth-grade year and had learned some pieces of the Gospels in Sunday school. They were like Aesop's fables, I thought: entertaining stories with a moral at the end. Be nice. Do good. Bring a friend to Sunday school. Mostly I remember being annoyed at my classmates, sixth-grade boys who giggled continually, looking for every chance to poke one another. I tried to do good, to be good, but God never came near. He remained distant, theoretical, deaf. I prayed for the heaviness we all carried in my family: that my father would get a job, that the kids at school would stop trying to beat me up, that there would be enough money to pay the electricity bill, that the bank wouldn't repossess the house. Never did I sense that I was heard, that God and I were in this together. I felt alone, bereft, stranded in a two-dimensional world while somewhere beat and pulsed the real world, where God lived, where love and colors and joy were possible, but just beyond my reach.

Now I knew why. I heard the gospel, the Good News that Jesus did in fact love me, and that he came to take on my sins—every one of them—to nail them to the cross, so I could go free. He came to make me his daughter! At the party, I heard the youth leader read the words from John: "I am the way, and the truth, and the life; no one comes to the Father but through Me."[7] The Father? I desperately needed a father! My father took not the slightest interest in his family, and worse, inflicted physical and emotional harm upon us as well. When the pastor asked us all to bow our heads at the end, to raise our hands if we wanted to "accept Jesus as our Savior," I was already there. My hand was already up. My sister raised her hand too.

And so it began. The leaving. I did not tell anyone what I had done when I got home that night. I knew they wouldn't understand, nor would they be terribly interested. We had far too many daily crises to worry about matters of the Spirit. I became heavily involved in a youth group in our town. Later, I chose to go to a Christian college, though my family didn't approve. Some saw me as a fanatic, a religious nut. I'm sure I was. But I knew God was leading me. I knew I was no longer alone. Then the day came, at seventeen, when I actually left for a college a thousand miles away in someone else's car and didn't look back. I knew I would never come back to live in New England again.

At that college I met Duncan, a disheveled Alaskan fisherman who was president of his class and ran the dorm. We married, still in school. Alaska would be my new home. Did I choose it in part because it was so far away? I think so. I was barely twenty. But the price of saying yes to Jesus and then to Duncan has been steep. My parents had no part in my faraway life. My children have not known their grandparents or their uncles, aunts, and cousins. There have been lovely visits, but also absences, long silences, hurt feelings, ruptured relationships.

We have no idea what will happen when we answer *Yes, I do, I will.* We do not dream that such a price will be asked. Is this what we all must do if we want to follow Jesus? Who can do this, pack up her life, leave her family, hit the Gospel Trail, wherever it takes her? I'm not sure this is required for all of us. Here is what I think *is* required: Jesus will show up in your life in some way: a man on the beach calling to you, a dream, words from the Scriptures, a friend who won't stop caring about you, a last-minute provision, the disappearance of the cancer cells, the fall down the cliff that didn't kill you, the forgiveness you didn't deserve from your son—all of them some form of miraculous catch. All of them some sort of glimpse of the crazy, inexplicable abundance and love of Jesus. Because it comes to you when you least expect it. It comes to you when you least deserve it. We can revel in the fish, in the dream, in our new health, in the love of a friend, a son, but none of that will be enough for long. None of that will sustain for long. We have to know—who did this? Who has this kind of mastery over disease? What is the source of this wisdom? Where does this love come from? We have to know, because somehow we know that here, *here*, is life itself, the life we have longed for but could not even name.

A call comes to every man and woman and child. We have all been called. We must follow to find out who it is that calls us, and what we have been called to. James, Andrew, Simon Peter, and John, and all the others did not yet know either one: what they would be doing or even who it was who had called them. They had no idea what "fishing for men" meant. They didn't even know who Jesus was for sure. But John the Baptizer seemed to know. And it appeared that maybe the fish in their sea knew him too. That was enough to start. Only one thing mattered now. This man, who could be "the lamb of God," has chosen them:

Come, follow me. Do not be afraid.

And he has chosen us as well:

Come, follow me. Do not be afraid.

CHAPTER FIVE

A FISH OR
A SNAKE?

On the third day a wedding took place at Cana in Galilee. . . .
When the wine was gone, Jesus' mother said to him, "They have
no more wine." . . . The master of the banquet tasted the water that
had been turned into wine. . . . Then he called the bridegroom aside
and said, "Everyone brings out the choice wine first and then the
cheaper wine after the guests have had too much to drink; but you
have saved the best till now."

JOHN 2:1, 3, 9-10

Ask and it will be given to you; seek and you will find; knock and
the door will be opened to you. For everyone who asks receives; the
one who seeks finds; and to the one who knocks, the door will be
opened. Which of you, if your son asks for bread, will give him a
stone? Or if he asks for a fish, will give him a snake? If you, then,
though you are evil, know how to give good gifts to your children,
how much more will your Father in heaven give good gifts to those
who ask him!

MATTHEW 7:7-11

WE'RE A MONTH into the fishing season now. I am out tonight on the ocean with my daughter, Naphtali. She is here for just three weeks, between summer internships at theatres down south. She is in the middle of a master of fine arts for theater directing. It's a slow night on the water. I'm thankful. But it's a jellyfish night, or rather, a jellyfish week. The ocean is thick and mucus-y with them, these *Aurelia aurita*, moon jellyfish, the clear kind that look like ocean water plus Knox Gelatine, with a little hyphenated cross as its entrails. Their omnipresence doesn't stop the work. Naphtali, her hair bound in a bandana, her huge green eyes vivid in a deeply tanned face, concentrates on the net. She motors the skiff forward through the net, as a steady stream of jellies slop through the bow roller into the skiff. The floor of the skiff is now just a mass of congealed water and little broken crosses I have to stand on and in.

I don't mind these. They feel somewhat antiseptic, and even holy, with a holy-ghost body. But other jellyfish come with them, these giant glops of oranges, pinks, rusts, as large as sinks, even bathtubs at times, their stinging strings like snot trailing behind. They're bagged in the net, and as we move forward, they'll slide into the boat, at my feet, and travel the length of the skiff. We lift our hands as they pass, narrow our eyes to protect our faces and skin from errant splashes of acid until each one disappears off the stern with a slurp. Sometimes one of us will get enough in our eyes to leave the nets and go ashore, slogging painfully up the hill to the house and the medicine shelf, where the eyewash waits.

The tide is twenty-one feet today, which means everything in the water, including us, is stretched taut as wires. "Catch it!" Naphtali shouts at me over the sound of the outboard. We've just rounded one of the buoys, and I should be leaning over the side of the skiff right now, with my arm hanging like a crane to snatch the net. I wasn't watching, though that's my job as bowman. I'm not as attentive as I should be in the skiff. Sometimes I'm sorting through decades of summer and work here; every fish that noses over the bow and into the skiff comes laden with history, generations of fish before it.

But the line is partially submerged, the corks underwater instead of floating on top. Either the tide is just a killer today, sucking the net, corks and all, underneath its strong arm, or the net is caught on something near the bottom.

"I can't reach it!" I call back to Naphtali. "The corkline is sunk!" She throttles down and reverses slowly, both of us surveying the problem. The corks are sunk for about five fathoms, around thirty feet.

"The net must be caught on a rock," Naphtali says from the stern. I nod, arms propped on the skiff sides, leaning over to see as far into the water as I can.

It's not uncommon for this to happen on the highest of tides. Most of our nets sit on sandy bottom, but some are set among rocks and boulders. But it's our bad luck that it has happened on our watch. Brute strength and a ferocious hand on the throttle of the outboard is the usual remedy.

"You wanna try it?" I ask, dubious. I get discouraged with all this: jellyfish, rocks, the tide, all of which are obstacles to what should be a fairly simple task: retrieving salmon from the nets. Fishing is so much harder than I imagined all those years ago. And what will we do in response? Tonight I want to do nothing. "Let's let the men on the next pick take care of it!" I suggest to Naphtali. I want to add, "Big, muscle-y, college-aged

men, as opposed to us." But this is just the wrong tactic to take
with her.

"No, we have to try," Naphtali says, her jaw set. "We're losing fish over the top of the net."

I sigh in concession. How have our roles reversed so utterly
and quickly?

I remember a day in the skiff twelve years before, when Naphtali
was fourteen. She was standing in the bow, where I am standing
now, and I was running the outboard in the stern.

"Mom, could I run the skiff for the rest of the pick?"

"Sure," I replied instantly, my eyebrows rising. She never
wanted to run the boat. Little wonder. Just starting a sixty-
horsepower outboard with a pull crank takes great strength.
Most women I know can't do it. I could do it, with the deft use
of my weight and some biceps, so Naphtali knew that she could
too. Starting the engine was hard enough, but maneuvering the
boat around swirling nets in the open ocean with winds and
constant tidal surges took finesse, fearlessness, and strength.
And the one who runs the motor runs the crewmen in the
bow—men who would be as much as ten years older than her.
Duncan had been pressuring her to this higher responsibility,
but she had resisted. Until now.

"Wanna take it now?" I shouted over the engine, careful to
keep my face neutral. We were heading to the next net, the bow
plunging between waves. She nodded her head and made her
way back between the totes and skiff sides.

Naphtali now stood in my place in the stern. I moved to the
center of the skiff. She gripped the outboard handle tentatively
and used her body as I do, as a stabilizer for the left arm. The

men don't need to do this; they have enough body weight and mass to absorb the intense vibration and the force of propulsion. As we approached the next net, she slowed.

We came in for the landing on the net, and I saw we weren't going to make it. The wind was pushing us over the line.

"Sorry!" she called as she reversed.

"That's okay! Let's go again!" I replied, facing out to the water, not watching her, giving her room.

We approached again. She slowed the engine, idled us close to the corks, and shifted into neutral for me to lean over the skiff side and lift the net out of the water, but we were still five feet short.

"ARRRGG! Which way do you turn this for reverse, Mom?"

"The other way. Turn it the other way!"

She turned the arm sharply toward herself, but we turned the wrong direction.

Again we missed. Just feet short, the wind blustered the bow over the other side of the corks.

"Mom, maybe you should do it!" Naphtali called, frustrated.

"No. You can do it." I would not tell her again how to do this, I decided. This was a knowledge that came not from language or shouted directives; it came only through the hands, the shift of her feet. I knew she would learn.

When we were finally done with our last net, Naphtali made one more request: "Mom, can I take it to the tender?" I smiled imperceptibly, not wanting to overreact. Driving the skiff to the tender is a small moment of triumph. The pick is over. You're delivering your harvest, the fruit of your labor, to the larger boat that will collect and then motor your catch to the processing plant. When we off-load, the salmon are weighed.

We'll know exactly, to the pound, how much we have caught. This feels like a measuring of your own worth. How hard did you work? How good are you? Our totes are half full this pick. It's a decent showing.

But this was even more momentous. She was driving to the tender instead of me. "Sure, go ahead." She tightened her grip on the outboard handle, stood straighter, and rounded the corner of the island, face set in stoic confidence, the "stern face" her father wears, her grandfather wore, all the men wear as they command their vessel from the stern. The face I wear as well.

We headed for the *Sierra Seas*, the larger boat that takes our fish and delivers them to the cannery. The other skiffs from our fishing operation were there, six of them, with two crewmen in each, all tied together waiting to off-load their fish. We saw them before they saw us. This was it—center stage. I glanced up at Naphtali, frozen in an inscrutable aplomb. Then they heard us and glanced in our direction. She was ready. This was her debut, her coming out. The Alaskan fishergirl's equivalent of a southern girl's debutante ball. It was public now—Naphtali is running the skiff. Everyone sees and knows. She is no longer a child or a crewman or a girl; she is a fisherman.

I was proud of her that day, but I wondered as well, *What am I giving to you, daughter?* Though most of her training was under her father's eye and hand, I was part of this too. What was I passing on to her? A skill that will bring her deeper into the heart of fishing than she has ever been. Running a skiff makes you captain of a small ship, presiding over one or two crewmen. It means you earn the right to travel your boat straight into a convulsed, tide-ripping storm of ocean and, in the midst of that storm, to fish and work as if there were none. It means you will hold other people's lives in your hands. It means you will work eight to fifteen hours every day through every summer. It means she will be a girl in a world of men, and expected to work like a man. And so it has been.

At fourteen, she was the only female out on the water every day, at all hours. At sixteen, she ran her own boat, training and giving orders to new crewmen five to ten years older than her. At seventeen, the year after our "Humpy Hell" season, she wanted to quit after the first week. Her words to me then, "I can't do this anymore," dropped a stone into my already heavy pocket. I had no words to cheer her for the three months ahead. She knew what was coming, how every day would play out, but we needed her. She needed the money for college. She couldn't quit or leave. She did not choose this life. It was chosen for her.

What are we passing on to you? I wondered that day and many days after. Is this bread or a stone, a fish or a serpent? Every parent wonders what they are handing to their children. In my first ten years out here, I asked myself continually, *What have I done? What is this life I have chosen?*

I arrived at twenty, from the backwoods of New Hampshire. I was used to chopping wood, hauling water, building houses, living without heat, but soon I was in another world. Duncan taught me how to pilot a small skiff through forty-knot winds, leaning over nets so full of fish we could not lift them from the water. We picked them in the water, then, throwing hundreds, thousands behind us into our skiffs for days. And there were nights Duncan asked me to drive a skiff full of fish around an island and a reef in the black dark, not knowing where the rocks were, and still going, praying and sometimes crying along the way. And the many nights we could not speak to each other for the fatigue and the distance between us.

I should have looked ahead to see all this when I first came, when I chose this life. But I didn't. I couldn't. I didn't know. And I in turn have passed this life on to my sons and my daughter. If I had thought about being a mother someday and passing a heritage on to my daughter, I would not have imagined this—the two of us out in a skiff, in orange rain gear, slimed by fish guts, blood, and kelp, the mountains and ocean rising up around us. I would not have imagined us killing fish instead of garnishing them; snatching salmon from watery jaws, shouting sea lions away from our nets, picking kelp at midnight, assessing a man's worth by body size and strength. I grew up with five siblings and a mother who built houses, fireplaces, and furniture, with a father mostly absent. No one spent much time in the kitchen, but somehow, in a rosy glow, I place Naphtali and me there.

There we are, within warm buttery walls, surrounded by appliances with dashboards and buttons just waiting to be controlled by the lift of our fingers. Engines that whirr to life with a touch rather than a full-body yank on a six-foot pull cord. We are wearing matching aprons instead of matching rain gear. Standing side by side while I demonstrate the roll of the pin, the fold of the dough instead of the slashing of kelp and the roll of jellyfish from the nets. Betty Crocker is there. We speak of literature, *Heart of Darkness*, *The God of Small Things*, as we braid a mound of challah. I teach her the science of yeasts and piecrusts, the brilliance of Indian curries. She learns to savor the artistry of food as I do, the unending beauty of colors and textures and flavors—this, the only domestic art that I love.

None of this has happened. The world I have given her, and the world she has made of what has been given, is entirely different. Naphtali enters the kitchen only to eat. Instead, when I can leave my other labors, writing and the work of a house and children, I gear up, join her, and head out to sea.

I don't know how long she'll keep returning. After grad school, maybe she'll never return. The thought of being alone here with all boys and men saddens me. But tonight, as I watch her in the skiff, I am amazed. She works quickly, surveying the way the net is hanging, the position of the running line, the tidal currents, the wind . . . In an instant she knows what to do and tells me in clipped sentences what she expects of me. "Don't roller it—tide's too strong. Put the longer pole in the bow. Grab the running line." She is competent, strong, fearless.

Is it possible that even the stones are a form of abundance? Is it possible that even the hard things that come to us are meant, finally, for our good? I know I have gained courage and strength out here. I have been pushed beyond my body's limits and past every boundary I knew of. I am still here, pulling heavy lines, admiring the beauty of the salmon, rolling in the grass on the hillside, turning every berry and rose into jams and jellies for my children. And here I am tonight. Though I am nearly sixty, I am out working on the ocean with my daughter.

But in the Gospels the fishermen and followers of Yeshua don't know yet what is before them. In walking after this rabbi, they know what they have given up—they've defied all societal and familial expectations for their lives. All that Zebedee wanted, and all that most fishermen want, is this: for their sons to carry on their trade. But now, these strong sons of his at the height of their powers—they are leaving? They are leaving to follow around after a rabbi?

Andrew and Simon Peter had to feel it too, the loss to their own father and the cost to themselves in the leaving. Now, what is it exactly that they have chosen? Have they given up the fish in their hands for a serpent? I know that this is not just metaphor. It would really happen, that the fishermen would haul in their nets from the lake and sometimes a water serpent—poisonous—would be caught among the fish. Some of them thought this man was the Messiah they were wait-ing for. Was this possible? There had been other claimants to this title—revolutionaries, each ending in disaster and death, crushed by the Romans. Would this one be the bringer of life or death? They did not know. They could only follow, watch, and hope.

And nothing was what they expected. Their first stop, a wedding. Water turned magically into wine. Simon Peter and Andrew might have been scandalized. "*This* is the miracle? *This* is the Messiah's power? We've left our father high and dry for this? We need him to restore the Temple, save our people—and instead he saves the host embarrassment for running out of wine?" Simon is ready for battle, not a wine tasting at a wedding. Andrew wants to see the Roman Empire collapse, wants its ruin. Wine? John longs for the days of fasting and atonement, when the people mourn over their sin. Wine? The Kingdom of God is coming, and this is what we get—wine? A wedding? Feasting? Dancing? It was easier to see the Kingdom through a shouting bearded man in a hairy tunic than this rau-cous wedding party. What have you given us, rabbi?

Not long after the wedding, they are sitting on a gentle

hillside with thousands, more than anyone wanted to count, of the sorriest mass of villagers from around the sea. Jesus seems to collect them, the ones every other leader ignores, the kind of followers no one else wants: the sick and weeping, the lame and palsied. It could not have happened, but it does—the mute wagging their tongue to sing! Crooked legs made straight! The blind watching the flight of a hawk! It's a riot there on the hill for hours! The start of a revolution? But then, what is this? This man they are following, who did all this, do they hear him? He speaks there on the hillside as if he is in the synagogue.

They cannot believe his words at first:

Blessed are the poor in spirit. . . . Blessed are those who mourn. . . . Blessed are the meek. . . . Blessed are those who hunger and thirst for righteousness. . . . Blessed are the pure in heart . . . the peacemakers. . . . Blessed are those who are persecuted. . . . Blessed are you when people insult you. . . . Love your enemies.[1]

What is this? Peter and James, John and Andrew wonder. This does not sound like a triumphant Messiah! And maybe a few of them feel a growing confusion. *Don't bless our need, our emptiness and poverty. Don't tell us this is blessing. Change it! Take it away! Just like you fixed all those legs and hands and eyes. Don't bless this poor, pitiable mess that we've become. We're your people—Israel! Fix us! Don't tell us to love the Romans, who hate us! Be our king and vanquish our enemies!*

But he went on, his words burning in their ears. Every now and then, the disciples glance around at the others. They too are rapt. Every sentence new, unexpected. They recognize these words: "You have heard that it was said . . ." Nearly all of them there on the hillside have memorized the words of the Torah, about adultery, taking oaths, divorce, an eye for an eye. But this teacher has changed the words. He has changed the endings. He doesn't do as the Pharisees do, who tighten the noose around every command from God to extrude it and make it smaller, harder, and longer. To make it a point of argument, generating debate and haggling over the tiniest of details. This man opens up the words to make them larger, generous, capacious even, opening up a meaning that penetrates straight to their hearts: *give him your other cheek to strike as well, give him your cloak also, do not worry about your life, love your enemies, pray in secret, forgive their debts, do not judge.*

Matthew's Gospel says that everyone who heard these words were astonished.[2] Astonished! This man is teaching with authority! But he has not studied under any of the known teachers of the Law. He has not gone all the way through the synagogue school! How can this be? No one has spoken the words of God this way before. No one has revealed their heart as this man has! But—there must be fear as well. These words go deeper; they are harder. *What is this Kingdom you're giving us, Yeshua? Love our enemies? Here, strike my other cheek too? Here, take my last cloak?* There are so many verbs in these sentences. They are not just words to know, to memorize, to rattle off when quizzed by rabbis or parents. These are words they are supposed to *live and do.* This teacher is different. He is asking more from them than they realized at first.

And later, after those words, where did he eat and drink, whom did he consort with but the worst of men and women:

traitorous collectors of taxes, colluders with the Romans. Prostitutes, sinners, those as broken on the inside as the ones broken on the outside on the hillside hospital that day. Some of them saw: He was living these words in ways they had never witnessed before.

Would anyone have recognized this yet, that maybe this new world was a place of such surfeit, such unending provision, such upside-down bounty that what is given up and given away is not lost? That maybe heaven was beginning right now, and meekness was winning, the persecuted were blessed, the reviled were loving their revilers? They saw Yeshua do all of these things! So many parties and feasts! When I raised my hand that day in the white country church and said, "Pick me, Jesus!" and when I followed him here to this island, the Alaska sky and mountains and sea were so vast and clean, so full of breath and drama, my hopelessness was washed away. And after the wedding, the disciples followed Jesus to that hillside, where a ward of wounded, sorry, hungry, limping people thronged, and they were healed, the worst and best of them. This teacher did so much more than teach! No other rabbi did this—put hands on bodies and cure them whole! It was almost too good to be real, too good to trust, but there they were, all these giddy ones healed under his touch. No matter what came next, were not they *all* healed? Could anyone else have done this, ever? This shouting, laughing hillside then must be the "kingdom of God"!

And there I was, just over twenty, in a skiff beside my new husband and father-in-law, the three of us moving from net to net, pulling salmon from the depths of a green sea, fish so glittering our boat sparkled in the sun. Were we not all clothed as beautifully as the lilies? After every net, Duncan would lean his wet nose down to mine and kiss me, so glad I was now part of his world. And I kissed him back, this man who smelled of salt water and fish. I kissed him back—me, this girl learning how to love, becoming a wife and a fisherman and maybe even a follower of Jesus all at the same time.

Those fishermen and the other followers did not know yet what would come of their new life. They did not know exactly what this Kingdom would look like. They had some ideas. They knew the scrolls. They knew they were the persecuted and reviled. They prayed daily for God to return to his people and to restore their nation's fortunes and power. Nothing like that had happened yet, but already they were glad. Glad! Wine and healing! Dancing and running! Teachings with authority! All of us—the disciples, me, my daughter, all of us who raise our hands, who move our feet, who walk behind or beside him, there we are on the sea, in a boat, or on the hillside running with new, sturdy legs marveling—what is this new place? Even a wedding won't run out of wine, and a man who could be the Messiah tells us all to "ask, seek, and knock," that our Father will give us gifts just for the asking. Can heaven really be this open and this near?

And look, my daughter, at all that you can do. Look at all I have done and am not done doing. In this new Kingdom, even with stones in our pockets, cannot a jellyfish, or even a snake—still bring life? Have we not all been given bread and fish after all?

CHAPTER SIX

ROCKING THE BOAT

When they heard about all he was doing, many people came to him from Judea, Jerusalem, Idumea, and the regions across the Jordan and around Tyre and Sidon. Because of the crowd he told his disciples to have a small boat ready for him, to keep the people from crowding him. For he had healed many, so that those with diseases were pushing forward to touch him.

MARK 3:8-10

Again he began to teach beside the sea. And a very large crowd gathered about him, so that he got into a boat and sat in it on the sea, and the whole crowd was beside the sea on the land. And he was teaching them many things in parables, and in his teaching he said to them: "Listen! Behold, a sower went out to sow. And as he sowed, some seed fell along the path, and the birds came and devoured it. Other seed fell on rocky ground, where it did not have much soil, and immediately it sprang up, since it had no depth of soil. And when the sun rose, it was scorched, and since it had no root, it withered away. Other seed fell among thorns, and the thorns grew up and choked it, and it yielded no grain. And other seeds fell into good soil and produced grain, growing up and increasing and yielding thirtyfold and sixtyfold and a hundredfold." And he said, "He who has ears to hear, let him hear."

MARK 4:1-9, ESV

NAPHTALI IS LEAVING NOW, on her way to an internship in LA. I say good-bye to her on the beach. As she stands there in her XtraTuf boots, with her hair in a single fat braid and bandana, her backpack and duffel bag in hand, I give her a quick hug. We've had so many good-byes in the last eight years, we are good at it. But this day tears spring unexpectedly, and I hold on too long. Naphtali laughs kindly and pats me on the back as she pulls away. "I'll see you soon, Mumma. Maybe at Christmas," she comforts, and she is in the skiff, pulling away into the rest of her life.

She must go. I don't want to keep her. But in her five-minute absence as I stand watching the skiff disappear, I decide I need to go out fishing more. That's where my children are. But who shall I go with? Who can keep company with me in the boat? I know instantly: Abraham and Micah. The older boys, like Duncan, don't talk much as they work, but the younger ones, thirteen and eleven, still love to talk in the skiff. Abraham can give an extensive movie or book review at the drop of a hat. Micah can critique Abraham's critique. And then there are the word games: Rhyme Out, Inkity-Pinkity.

But I hesitate. Fishing with the boys means I'll be going out with Duncan as well. Which means I'll be breaking my own rule: *Don't fish with Duncan.* I made that rule for myself—and for Duncan and our marriage—more than twenty-five years ago, and I've kept it religiously. But tonight I soften. I believe in the possibility of fresh starts and renewal. And we are both so much older and wiser now. I wait for the right moment, just before dinner.

"Duncan, how about if I go out with you and the boys tonight?" I say casually.

"Really?" He looks at me with surprise. "Are you sure? There's a pretty big swell from yesterday's blow, you know."

"Yeah, I know. It'll be fine. I just want to spend time with you and the boys."

Duncan shrugs, which I interpret as a yes, and off we go to get ready.

I join Abraham and Micah in the gear shed.

"You're going out with us, Mom?"

"Yeah. Is that okay?"

"It's kind of stormy still. Hey, maybe you can take my place?" Abraham looks hopefully into my face.

"No, you can go for me!" Micah chips in. "I'm the youngest. You should take my place!"

"We'll all go together. It'll be fun!" I smile at them reassuringly while pulling on my rain pants, then adjusting my life jacket. Then I think about the word *fun*. It's hardly fun for them anymore. But maybe I can bring a little variety and entertainment for them this pick.

We clunk heavily out of the shed in all our orange vinyl gear, wrapped nearly head to toe, and onto the gravelly beach. My eyes turn again to the water and the skiff we're pulling ashore. This will be our home this evening—a tin can, arrowed in the front, the sides plastered with pieces of kelp riding on grey swells, textured with wind. I'm ready. Duncan joins us on the beach. We shove off, leaping over the side as we reverse into the deep water. It feels good to be going out together.

During the first hour, I join the boys in the bow to help with picking fish and lifting the lines. The ocean is sloppy, but the island protects us for the first three nets. By the time we get out to the Seal, the net out in the open ocean, with no protection, the swells are rolling in with intention, driven by a southeast wind. Micah is slowing down, closing his eyes for a second or two then opening them slowly. He's seasick. I know we have at least three more nets to go. My own stomach is fluttering, but if I take deep breaths and keep my eyes steady on the mountains as I pick fish, I'll be all right.

"Micah, look at the mountains," I urge. "Keep your eyes on something stationary. That will help."

"I know," he mumbles, as he holds the cork line.

We are standing side by side in the bow, facing the rolling water, our bodies rising and falling in that terrible lurching pattern that squirms my stomach and saps my strength. Micah lets go of the net and sits down heavily on the shelf in the bow, his head hanging down.

"Micah, keep your head up! Keep your eyes up!"

"I don't want to," he grumbles.

"Then just stand up and take some deep breaths." Some of the swells are breaking on the side of the skiff as we sit sideways on the net. We're showered with spray every minute or so, matching our rise and fall.

I want to take him in to shore, back to the island. He's eleven. He's a tough kid who's never been babied, but he's still my baby, and all my mother heart wants to do is take care of him.

"C'mon, Micah. It will help. Really!" I try one more time.

Duncan hears my rising voice, looks up from the fish he is picking. "Micah!" he shouts from the stern. "Come on back here and lie down on the seat."

I look at Micah with concern. He looks like he's about to throw up. "Just breathe deeply, Micah, and lift your head."

Duncan frowns at me. "He just needs to lie down. Micah! Get back here and just lie down!" he calls again, forcefully.

I know he's going to get mad if I speak again. I know his rules, that the skipper's words are unquestioned, but this is my youngest son. I didn't stop being a mother when I stepped into the skiff. This is one reason we moved to another island—so we would stop separating our lives and roles this way. I take a deep breath and try one more time.

"He'll just feel worse."

"Just shut up, Leslie!" Duncan yells now. "I don't want to hear another word. I know what to do. Micah gets sick all the time." He glares at me with his jaw set defiantly. Then in a softer voice, "Come on back here, Micah. I've got a spot right here for you. And you get back here and sit, Leslie." He shoots me another dagger.

I clamp my jaw shut and remain standing, my hand on the tote to balance in the swells. I'm so angry I want to jump overboard and swim home. In a flash it all comes back—why this doesn't work, Duncan and me in a skiff together. We're husband and wife until we step into the skiff. Then we are skipper and crew, boss and hireling.

I remember my first year here, even my first time climbing into a skiff. The boats then were small eighteen-foot wooden boats, yet whoever ran the outboard engine in the stern was the undisputed master and king. It didn't bother me then. What did I know about skiffs and oceans and engines? I was happy to submit to the lifelong knowledge of others.

I was happy to change my vocabulary and speech patterns as well. Because this seems to be required. Words are used differently out on the water. Words in the boat are sparse, so each one weighs more heavily than words on land. Nearly every word used is attached to an object: running line, buoy, anchor, snitter, stern, hook, gaff. Verbs are still important—"untie the line," "coil the bowline," "tie off the running line"—but the emphasis is always on the nouns and always on the silent subject *you*. Which meant all of these are orders, commands. Adverbs, adjectives, and abstractions are entirely irrelevant to our work in the boats.

I learned to translate and speak that new terse shorthand, which was remarkably bereft of any of the philosophizing and discussions Duncan and I loved so much. Here Duncan would say to me, "Put the skiff on the buoy. Tie an anchor hitch and a bowline. Then we'll go put out the other net." Or, "Pull up to the lead line." Three minutes later, I'm huffing from the effort. "Okay, hook it there." A few minutes later, "Don't lose that red" as I grab a red salmon slipping through the net. These utterances were so different from our conversations in college and grad school, which were exchanges rather than commands, when we might ask each other, *Is predestination the same as foreknowledge and election? How can God hold us responsible if we don't really have free moral agency?* Or, *Do you think it's possible to be a theistic existentialist?*

But in the skiff, nothing was up for discussion or debate. You cannot argue with the skipper or present another option, no matter how absurd or impossible the command. I know it makes sense some of the time. We're afloat in an element that can kill us in minutes. Order must prevail. And the work must get done. Regimented hierarchy has always been the maritime way, for good reason. But I rebel. When I am running the skiff, I let others speak. I do not yell. The crewman does not work *for* me; we work together. And when the crew are my sons, and one son is sick, and the skipper is my husband, cannot some of that authority be relinquished?

I fume and keep my eyes on the whitened waters, on Abraham, as we work together in the bow. I silently renew my vow: *I will not go out fishing with Duncan again. Ever.*

A few months later, on fresh waters instead of salt, I am granted strange moments of authority in a boat much bigger than our skiffs. It is my third night on my hike around the sea. I plan on crossing the lake that morning on one of the larger passenger boats. I will cross and land in Ginosar to see the "Jesus boat" in the museum and then hike the four hours to Tiberias that day. But I wake up twenty minutes late. In a panic, I stuff my nightclothes into my backpack, splash water on my face, brush my teeth, and run down to the dock just in time to see the stern, with *Faith* in bold letters, sailing away. I recognize it as one of the "holy boats" harbored in Tiberias. The whole fleet of them look like mini versions of Noah's ark. There it goes, with an American flag snapping from its rigging, and "The Star-Spangled Banner" blaring through a loudspeaker. I sigh.

I watched these boats in Tiberias every day, coming and going, loading and unloading with scores of pilgrims from around the world. The boat companies, knowing who is coming and the country they hail from, will blast a recording of their national anthem while raising that nation's flag as they edge out of the harbor. Just a few mornings before, I had seen a group from Africa board the boat named *Love*. About one hundred people stepped on board to the beat of worship music, erupting into dancing, rhythmic leaping, and clapping, bodies pressed together like a rave, hands up in ecstatic worship before the boat even set off. No one is dancing on this American boat.

An official-looking man with a walkie-talkie approaches me. I turn to him, hopeful. "That's my ride. I made a reservation. Can you call it back?"

"Yes, no problem," he says in perfect English, and with just a few words of Hebrew, Noah's ark swings around slowly. The scratchy recording on cheap speakers ruptures the quiet morning: "Gave proof through the night that our flag was still there. Oh, say, does that star-spangled ba-an-ner-er ye-et wa-ave . . ."

I know in a second, as the faces come near, who my fellow travelers are: the group of young people I saw swimming in the lake last night. I had caught the logo on several of their backpacks: BYU. I am already disappointed by this whole small venture. I'm like most travelers. When I'm overseas, I'm not interested in hanging out with my fellow countrymen. But I have to get across the lake.

I stand on the dock awkwardly as the boat nears, everyone's eyes on me, the errant final passenger traveling alone. As the boat docks, I step on the railing and climb over, met with a young man's helping hand.

"Thank you! I'm sorry to be late and to make you turn around!" I say to all the clean-faced students looking at me with curiosity.

"Where are you from?" someone asks me.

"I'm from Alaska. How about you?" Though I already know.

"We're all from BYU," an older man steps forward to say. He's about my age. A professor, perhaps? Then, "Alaska? I'm from Alaska!" A young man with short black hair and a round face emerges and smiles at me.

"Where 'bouts?" I ask. "I'm from Kodiak."

"Kodiak? Cool! I'm from Delta Junction."

"Really? That's amazing." I look around. Everyone is smiling at our little reunion. I don't know him, of course. Delta Junction is a tiny village about four hundred miles from Kodiak. But the mood is set. Everyone is cheerful, and they are all also, I notice, young and beautiful in more than the usual way, the way that all young people are. They look pure, somehow. The girls are dressed modestly in skirts and blouses, the boys all with short haircuts and collared shirts. Just like my college days at a Midwest Christian college. But I'm the odd woman out, I realize. I'm neither clean nor neat. My shorts are dirty and my legs are scratched up and bruised from stumbles through bamboo thickets and on boulders on and off the barely marked trail.

We all smile a little too brightly at one another now as the boat engines rev up again and we swing away from the dock. I settle on a wooden bench next to an older woman and a student. I discover that these students are in Israel for the semester, some for the entire year, studying in Jerusalem. They're here in Galilee on a special weekend trip.

Ten minutes into the crossing, to my surprise, the engine stops and the boat drops anchor. The man who first greeted me when I boarded now stands up on the upper deck with a microphone in his hand. All eyes turn to him.

"Good morning, ladies and gentlemen," he says pleasantly, smiling as he looks around at his already quiet and expectant audience. "Well, here we are. On the Sea of Galilee. Would you take out your Bibles and turn to Matthew? We're going to look at some special passages in the Gospels."

My eyes go big. Of all the groups I would happen to cross

with, somehow it's them. The students eagerly open their Bibles and pull out notebooks. The professor begins to read the passages, not just about the calling of the fishermen, but the calming of the storm, Jesus' walking on water, all the passages I am examining while here. He gives an overview on fishing in Jesus' time. I listen carefully while the students frantically scribble notes. He mispronounces some words and gets a few details about fishing wrong. Then he ends with a brief homily about answering Jesus' call and following him wherever he takes us.

I sit on the hard bench, smiling through the whole message, amazed at God's providence and timing. But also troubled. Everything he said could have been said by a pastor of a Protestant or Catholic church. Indistinguishable. Yet I'm not sure if my new friends see Christ as I do, as not only the Son of God, but God of very God himself. Which is why he was shouted onto the crucifixion cross. When the homily is over, I approach the professor and introduce myself in more detail, telling about this project and my little hike around the Sea. His face lights up. "Here, tell everyone what you're doing!" he says, and without hesitation thrusts the microphone, still on, into my face.

"Uhhhhhh," I stumble, surprised, mic to mouth. I speak in front of people all the time, but I wasn't prepared for this. I am almost halfway through my trip, but I have no pat answers, no huge epiphanies yet to report. What will I say? I take a breath and begin. "Uh, hi again, everyone." The students all turn from their conversation groups to look at me with curiosity. "Your prof just gave me the mic so I can tell you what I'm doing here. He thought you might be interested."

And I begin, telling about the hike, about this book, about my life in Alaska, our fishing life, what I know about fishermen.

I get into the calling of the fishermen, and I hear myself getting preachy and breathy, creating a cadence and dramatic pauses: "Fishermen don't leave their nets, ladies and gentlemen! They just don't. There must have been something incredibly compelling about Jesus that they did it—just walked away from their nets and their family and the life they had always known. I tell you, my husband would never leave his nets. When you grow up with it, it's in your blood. But clearly Jesus was no ordinary man. Jesus was no ordinary rabbi." And on I go, the young people listening, me not knowing from one minute to the next exactly what I'm going to say. But finally I am done. They break into applause.

What have I just done? I've just preached the gospel to a boatload of beautiful Mormon kids in the middle of the Sea of Galilee. How did I get this authority? They listened to me because I'm from Alaska, because I know a little bit about fishing and boats and nets. How ironic, I smiled to myself. I have little authority on my home waters, but those very waters give me authority on these.

Later, in my hotel room that night, I marvel that this woman from Alaska spoke the gospel on the very waters Jesus himself sailed and taught upon. I wonder, too, did they hear me? Did they hear somewhere among my stumbling words the truth about Christ? Was I sowing good seeds?

I wonder, too, how well the crowds listened to Jesus that strange day when he too spoke from a boat. A rabbi, sitting and teaching from a boat? What a mixed-up day it was, like so many of those days. What was normal anymore? The men following Jesus could hardly remember. But they came to expect this—mobs. Everywhere they went, people gathered, collected into pressing masses of outstretched hands and open mouths clamoring to be seen and touched. This day, too, clusters of families and villagers gathered noisily around Jesus as he sat. He started out alone, just sitting near the lip of the water. Praying, maybe, or watching the boats on the lake in a moment of needed repose. Then here they came. They hadn't traveled as far as I or the BYU students did to be there, but they were searching too, like us. Surely it was the healings they were after! Of course! Wouldn't we all just scoop up our crippled grandmothers and blind daughters, our demon-possessed uncles and our mute brothers, and hustle them to the one man who's got the holy touch? So there they were, pushing and shoving one another to get closer. If they could only just reach him!

That day in the Gospels, most were hoping just to touch his cloak, but some were looking for more. They had heard the news: "Repent!" and "the kingdom of God" had reverberated through every Jewish home. It meant something was happening, or about to happen. That the yoke of the Romans would be loosened, maybe? That God's judgment was perhaps about to fall upon their enemies?

The twelve with him are excited this day, each one thinking, *Look at how the crowds are growing! We're gathering more and more around us every day! We're going to start the revolt and take back our nation from Rome! All the world will see and remember: We are God's chosen people!*

So much energy and force surrounds Jesus, hands reach out to grab his wrist, to touch a corner of his tunic, he knows this will not go well. He sees the boat sitting on the shoreline just thirty feet away. Maybe he is laughing and shooing the crowd, who shuffle their feet with him, over to the boat. Andrew is there with him, maybe, and John. He edges his way over, nods to the two fishermen, tipping his head out to the lake. All three give a shove on the wooden gunwales and throw their legs over as the boat glides onto water. Christ is clearly in command here. The people on shore are astounded. What is the rabbi doing? He's never done this before! The water is shallow here, shallow enough that John simply grabs an oar and poles the boat out until Jesus raises his hand to stop. Andrew catches the signal and throws out the anchor.

It's a strange, quiet moment. This onetime carpenter, now a kind of rabbi, has taken charge of this boat, acting like a captain. He's a man of the land, not of the sea! Some are saying he is Elijah come back. A few are even calling him "Messiah." Which means he belongs in the synagogue, not here on their beach where fish and merchants and shoppers and sellers meet and mingle, barter and argue. It's a crazy day full of contradiction and paradox and hope.

They feel hope most of all, these legions of villagers along the shoreline, who finally drop their outstretched hands and now wait, all eyes on Jesus. Many of them were there the day of the long teaching on the mount and remarked at his unprecedented authority in the words of God. What will he do next? A hush falls, the hush of those hungry for healing, the hush of the disciples waiting for more displays of his power, the hush of those desiring incisive further understanding of the Scriptures. Into this quiet, he waits for the right moment and finally speaks:

Listen! Behold, a sower went out to sow. And as he sowed, some seed fell along the path, and the birds came and devoured it.[1]

We have to see this: The famous rabbi sits in a boat facing the crowd on the beach. He's in a boat, but he's not going anywhere: The boat is anchored. Then he tells the crowd, desperate for healings and miracles, a story about a farmer. A short story about a farmer and what happens to the little seeds he plants.

> Other seed fell on rocky ground, where it did not
> have much soil, and immediately it sprang up, since
> it had no depth of soil. And when the sun rose, it was
> scorched.[2]

But no one knows what he's talking about. Not even the disciples. Not even the farmers in the crowd. They recognize the truth of his words—yes indeed, seeds often fall in all the wrong places.

> Other seed fell among thorns, and the thorns grew up
> and choked it, and it yielded no grain.[3]

They are puzzled and disappointed. Maybe a few remember the prophets, Isaiah and Jeremiah, talking about seedtime and harvest as pictures of God redeeming his people. But most are confused. His followers especially. Yeshua has demonstrated more authority than anyone else they've ever known, but he seems to be inviting rather than ruling. The fishermen note that he's commandeered someone's boat, but he's telling stories rather than issuing commands. The people want healing, but he's giving them illustrations. The disciples want him to show off his power, but he's telling parables.

What is he doing? the twelve men must have wondered. *You've got it now,* they must have thought. *This audience! The whole world is coming after you, and surely you are the Messiah and they are all knowing it now too! Don't waste your authority! Now, bring them in! Say the words that will catch them, the way you did with us!*

Peter looks at Andrew, John looks at James, each one of them trying to discern from the others' faces some kind of meaning. Surely they should know, these twelve, after all these weeks of walking with him, walking beside and behind him? And all they've seen and heard? Why isn't he speaking plainly as he did on the hillside that day—all those words about giving your cloak, loving your enemies, "do not worry about your life"? Maybe one of the disciples wonders how it is that their teacher has sat so all can hear, but he does not speak so all can understand. Who has ears to hear this?

It's not that they've never heard parables before. They know and maybe remember a few parables from their study of the prophets, but these are different. They listen to every word with an array of feelings—curiosity, confusion, disappointment—but more than this, they *must* know what this story means. They have to know! Every word Yeshua has spoken since they've been together has mattered.

It's not until later that they find out. Later when everyone has left, when it's just Jesus, the Twelve, and some others, too—some other "followers," Mark's Gospel says.[4] They go into Peter's house and ask, sheepishly, but with hearts burning, "What does it mean, the parable about all those seeds?"[5]

Jesus is not entirely patient: "Don't you understand this parable? How then will you understand any parable?"[6] But then he tells them, quietly and gently unraveling the meaning plain and straight. "The seeds are the words of God," he says, looking intently at them.[7] This alone is unsettling: The news of heaven is a tiny seed? Why not a hammer! Or a sword! And then, the rest: Only one group of seeds out of the four groups planted will actually take root and bear fruit? This new Kingdom that is finally coming, when everything will be set aright, when all God's promises will be fulfilled and we'll be a nation again and God will be our God and king—and most of the seeds we sow will be scorched, choked out, plucked out, stolen by Satan? I can see them shaking their heads. No! This is bad news about the Good News of the Kingdom! Jesus assures them that his words will be heard and understood by "those who have ears to hear,"[8] but how many will this be? They look around the room: Out of that massive crowd, only a small group have followed him into the house to hear more.

When Jesus taught on the lake that day, he did indeed rock the boat. Nobody wanted to hear parables, I suspect, and least of all that one! They all wanted healings, the before-and-afters, the sick-made-well, all that drama. The disciples wanted Yeshua to showcase his power and shout a clear message over the crowds like John did. They wanted to hear that their teacher's words would be embraced and believed by all. What leader gathers converts by prophesying rejection? Yeshua surely was wasting his position and authority! He was not making "follow after me" easy.

I don't like that parable very much either, but I am grateful for it. I see its truth all around me still, these two thousand years later. I've watched friends, family, and neighbors who received the seed for a while, then tossed it out. My father once believed in God, but over the years he disavowed God. Someone else took up Buddhism. Another dropped out of church and left his wife and children for a mistress. Another who grew up in church and youth group rejected the biblical Jesus and constructed his own version of a savior. The seeds went out, but the cares of the world, their own worries, appetites, and desires, and the devil himself stole away the root and the fruit.

I saw it even that day in the boat crossing the Sea, with the lovely Mormon students who eagerly opened their Bibles to read about Jesus, who sang hymns about him there on the waters of Galilee, who studied his words—but did they have ears to hear that Christ *is* Immanuel, God with us, God of very God?

I don't like this parable this day especially. I don't like the truth of it in my own life. Those sharp words from Duncan in the skiff unleash my pride and a flood of memories that choke out my faith. I know the root of it: how many times I have been muted and invisible in the skiff and onshore as well. I see the crows circling, and I don't shoo them away. It scares me, how easily my own angry heart parches the soil. How quickly the weeds of worry and self-protection spring up. There's so much against the growth of that tiny seed! How will we ever make it? The Twelve must have wondered the same.

I know what I need to do. Even in the skiff, before the pick is over, I know Duncan and I need to talk. I know I need to let go. But my heart is still seething. I do want to follow Jesus. But not now. When the boat hits the beach two hours later, I leap out and march up the hill silent, alone.

CHAPTER SEVEN

MENDING THE WORLD

Once again, the kingdom of heaven is like a net that was let down into the lake and caught all kinds of fish. When it was full, the fishermen pulled it up on the shore. Then they sat down and collected the good fish in baskets, but threw the bad away. This is how it will be at the end of the age. The angels will come and separate the wicked from the righteous and throw them into the blazing furnace, where there will be weeping and gnashing of teeth.

MATTHEW 13:47-50

WE'RE HAVING A PARTY. Dinner's over and we're drinking hot chocolate, eating butterscotch pudding and peanut butter cookies, telling stories about the night. It was take-up night, when we pull all the nets from the ocean into the skiffs, and then out onto the beach for mending. We've been fishing continually for two weeks, night and day. Everyone is happy for a little time on shore. Duncan is celebrating in the other room, reading. I am here with the kids and crew. Micah crumbles his cookie into his hot chocolate. Elisha dunks it whole, gulping it down in a single bite. The evening on the water was calm, but there was a lot of kelp and jellyfish, slowing down the work.

"We could hardly get Russian Dick's net in last night," Elisha says, with neither complaint nor boast.

"We just hauled it all in, kelp, junk, everything," Isaac adds. "No way the washing skiff was going to get there in time."

"Arrrrgggggggg! Do I have to mend tomorrow?" Abraham moans, thunking his head dramatically on the table. "The nets are gonna be a mess." He fake cries. Everyone keeps dunking their cookies and slurping their hot chocolate. In the next moment, he raises his head. "Hey! I got a name for a boat!"

"Oh, not another one," Micah complains, his mouth full of whipped cream.

"The *Pickpocket*!" Abraham announces triumphantly. He's always happy with his ideas.

"Oh, like that wrecked boat in Larsen Bay?" Elisha asks.

"Nope. That was the *Pocket Robber*. Mine's better, and it gets a subtitle too: the *Pickpocket: It'll Scare the Dickens out of You!*" Groans all around.

"You must be reading *Oliver Twist* again," I say. "I like it!"

"Hey, we got two new songs." Elisha and Peter start singing

their sea shanties, composed in the skiff that day, one they made for mending net in the rain, and another for heading out into a storm, which is coming, the forecast says. Their voices rise discordantly, and they stand to offer hand motions while we laugh and applaud. It's past midnight, and morning and the nets will be here far too soon, but how can any of us let go of this cheer around the table?

The next morning everyone's on the nets early. Everyone but me.

I'm an hour late. I check the venison roast one more time. It's tucked neatly into the oven, surrounded by potatoes, carrots, and onions. Kristi made fudge cake and whole wheat rolls the night before. Everything should be ready by 1:00 p.m., when we stop for lunch.

I step into my boots, grab my coffee cup, and start my commute—a hundred steps down the steep hill to the beach, where the nets the color of ocean hang slack across the racks. It's a gorgeous day. The sky is mostly blue, and the mountains down the bay are hovering angelically over the calm waters. Even the mountains on the peninsula are visible, their glaciered peaks floating over the Shelikof Strait. My heart leaps. Over the years, I've spent enough time mending nets in the wind and rain. Some days were so cold we stood in winter coats, hoods up over our faces, our fingers barely able to move. Not today.

It's mid-July now. The early red salmon run in June was poor. Our hopes are still on the run of pink salmon, now clearly late but due to show up any day. We'll need a lot of them, though. The price has dropped to seventeen cents a pound, making each pink salmon worth about sixty cents. We can hardly catch enough to pay for the gas it costs to catch them.

But we'll take them. This year we need every salmon that finds its way to our nets. Which means that when our nets are pulled from the waters, we mend the holes and tears that lose us fish. Everyone would rather be fishing than mending, with at least the hope of catching fish and earning money. But if our nets are not repaired, our small catch will shrink yet further. We have seven nets to mend in three days.

As I approach the nets on the beach, Abraham and Micah, standing nearest the ocean, look up. I see last night's cheer is gone. They shoot me the look of victims under protest. This is their first year to mend, and they are already mourning their lost childhood. Up until this year, mending days were mostly play days for them. I smile at them encouragingly, signaling they would get little sympathy from me. Elisha and Isaac over on the other net give me a half-second look, then return to their handwork. They're tired from the late night and the work this week. I see it in their faces.

Duncan is down here too, I see, and Peter and Josh, each one standing fixed and solemn before the net, arms chest high as they paddle their hands through, carefully looking for holes. The sea-green webbing, made of monofilament, fabricated in Japan, is deceptively strong. But it is no match for our own propellers that get entangled; for the sea lions who come and swat salmon from it and swim through it; for the seals, even, who can pop through its fingers if they should ever come near. And these nets are tired and worn. I know it'll be slow going.

I avoid looking at Duncan. It's been four days since our fight in the skiff. I feel the growing chasm between us as memories and past hurts revive and line up in a chorus line. We're busy, on a schedule that doesn't relent. I'm content to let the ladies sing and dance right now, no matter how bitter and shrill their voices.

I go to the mending box and pick up the same accessories everyone else is wearing. Scissors that hang from twine around my neck—to cut out the ragged meshes. A white plastic needle about five inches long for my right hand, wound with green twine for sewing the torn meshes. And a flask of glue hung from a string that I'll hook onto my belt.

While I'm draping myself with these accouterments, an operatic voice cuts the sea air. "What's on?" I ask, unable to make out the voices yet.

"*Les Mis*," Abraham answers me across the net, with a victorious lift of his eyebrows. I smile back. He must have won the lottery today. It was Harry Potter on the last net-mending days, blaring from a boom box on the warehouse ramp, followed by a heavy dose of *Guns, Germs, and Steel* after that. Abraham and I have been lobbying for *Les Misérables* for several days. Valjean is singing right now. Valjean the forgiving one, the dispenser of mercy. I'd rather not listen to him right now. I'm on Javert's side today—Justice! Just give me justice!

Now, fully appointed, I find an untouched section of the net, between Abraham and Isaac. "Anyone mended here yet?" I ask. Six faces flash a no and I begin, but my heart sinks immediately. This net is wet, since they just pulled it out of the skiff this morning. And it reeks. Jellyfish in various stages of decomposition dangle in globs. Rockweed, grasses, and the tresses of bull kelp twine and drape through the meshes. I grimace at the jellyfish, some clear, some brownish. I could go get a pair of protective latex gloves like all the guys are wearing, and I should get a raincoat—I'm about to get slimed—but I don't want to take the time.

The nets are long and deep, some stretching fifty feet in depth. Some are six hundred feet long. It's more webbing than I want to calculate. I reach for the first blob of jellyfish with my bare hands and yank. It separates and slumps to the sand. One down. At least twenty more of these lie ahead of me. But my hands have already found the first hole. It's a big one. I keep pulling to find the end of it—there. A good five feet of mesh is gone, and the edges are tattered and ragged. All these frayed edges will need to be cut out and a patch sewn in from another net. This will be about a six-foot-by-five-foot hole, I guess, my heart sinking.

Valjean is singing bravely now from the speakers behind me. I hate to interrupt him, but I must. "Does anyone know what this is? A sea lion hole? Or a propeller hole?"

Duncan's on a big hole himself, I can see, and he's counting the meshes for the patch. His lips move silently. When he's done, he looks up at me with a frown. "Yeah, Isaac told me about that. It's a kicker hole. You want me to do it?" he says, with an edge.

He knows his offer is a kind of challenge to me. I sigh, knowing this will take at least an hour, working as fast as I can. "No, I can do it," I say without looking back.

This day could not be more beautiful or more tranquil. Four of my children are here. The peregrine falcons shriek overhead, kiting at the top of the mountain. The oystercatchers patrol the beach with soft hoots. Sea lions blast past us, snorting ocean through their nostrils.

I am glad to be here this morning, but I am not at peace. It's not just Duncan, though I am weary with my war against him. I'm thinking about my other family, still grieving an unspeakable loss that I don't know how to fix or change. And worst of all, the Mideast is blowing up again, I heard this morning on BBC. Christians are fleeing Syria still, tens of thousands of them. The persecution and exodus out of Iraq was appalling, and now Syria. I almost wish I hadn't listened. It's so much easier to block it all out, to ignore the satellite radio, to scroll past the images on my computer screen, to just live out here in the beauty and the work of this island thousands of miles from war.

But I cannot turn away. I saw the photos of Syrian children fleeing their homes with their families. I've seen footage of the destruction in Iraq. While in Israel, I spent the day with an Arab Christian family whose lives were directly affected by these events. They invited me in that day, fed me all day long, while I played with their three beautiful children. The news wears their faces now.

I stand at the nets, my chest tight. I know Jesus' yoke is light, but sometimes it feels heavy. I have found over the years that the gospel does not always simplify my life or the lives of any of his followers. If we are listening well, it rends us first. It shatters us. This new life with the Holy Spirit within pummels my heart as much as soothes it. He adjures us to love the unloved, to clothe the unclothed, to pray for those who persecute us. I am constantly rocked from self-sufficiency and determined ignorance into longing for others' freedom and healing.

Here is the paradox of the gospel: It brings peace and fellowship with God himself, but it doesn't allow us to be satisfied with our own good fortune. It awakens us to the world and its afflictions, and our own afflictions multiply because of it. For the disciples as well. Suddenly these twelve men awakened from their cultural slumber to feel great concern for women, for lepers, for prostitutes, for the unclean. Whole categories of people were swept from comfortable invisibility into their path, sometimes laid at their very feet.

I have no answers right now for any of this turmoil within my own house, my own family, and the wars around the world. But my hands do not hesitate. They know how to mend and sort without a thought. They know what to pull and toss out of the net, what doesn't belong. There will be ribbons of kelp, a twig or two, a piece of fish gut twisted into a knot through the mesh. On the lead line, I see a few sculpins entangled, rotting, waiting for our extraction. This is part of our work: We mend and sort, tossing out the useless, the once-living creatures now grotesquely dead. Here is Jesus' parable come to life on my own shores: The good fish are taken out of the net in the water, and the rest, all of this organic trash, will be raked into a pile and left for the eagles and gulls who will pick through the carrion with raucous fights and cries.

I see the parable in real life on the Sea of Galilee, too. I am at the hotel in Ein Gev run by the kibbutz, and discover that the one remaining seine boat on the lake is harbored there.

"I heard he's going out tomorrow morning. Do you want to go with them?" the receptionist asks as I check in that night.

"Oh, for sure!" I can't believe this luck.

Jenny, her name tag says, catches my enthusiasm and laughs. "Just be there at the dock by eight, and you can go. I'll let them know."

The next morning I stand awkwardly by the dock, watching two young men gather ice and snacks. A young woman shows up next, barefoot, in shorts. She is from Denmark, it turns out, and is here volunteering on the kibbutz for a month. Two more appear, both young men, one from Illinois, the other from the UK. Both Jewish, both living on the kibbutz for a year or two while they figure out their future. Their language of choice on board, they tell me as we begin, is "Hebrish," a jumble of Hebrew and English.

A crew of five works this thirty-five-foot boat, skippered by a young man in his twenties with chestnut hair, Asher, who directs the day's work and his international crew with quiet assurance.

We leave the dock by 9:00 a.m. It is another warm, sunny day, in the low eighties. The haze lifted this morning, so I can see the water and the surrounding hills with clarity. I wear shorts and sandals on the boat, as do the fishermen, which feels nearly scandalous to me. My Alaska fishing self both laughs and protests, *If you can work in sandals, is it really work?*

Asher slowly cruises the waters, watching the sonar, looking for fish. They are looking specifically for musht. It is nearly the end of the musht season, and the price is good, almost two dollars a pound. They hope to scoop up some final schools of the popular fish. "We have not been out for ten days, so I'm ready to catch some fish!" Asher nods to me, excited. I am ready too.

The first set goes out, the net forming a large, graceful circle, then is pulled in by hand, arm over arm. Hopefully a school is trapped inside. As the bottom of the net, the purse end, comes close, I lean over the boat with the crew, my camera trained on the "moneybag," the bottom of the purse seine that now holds whatever has been brought up from the deep. This is the moment that turns ordinary men and women into addicts.

After an hour of cruising the waters, watching the sonar, and now almost an hour in making the set, what will they get? What creatures from the dark waters will now be theirs? How many fish, what kind, and how much money will they pocket? How many bills can be paid?

Four of them strain to muscle the last of the net out of the water. I am determined to record this moment. When the net finally comes in, it happens. One of those moments I could not have planned. The parable unfolds before me. The catch is fairly small, but they dump it into the nearby skiff, three heads bent, and arms begin to sort it quickly, efficiently, their hands knowing exactly what fish goes where. Five kinds of fish came in. Asher narrates this little drama for me and my camera.

"These are musht. This is good. We got a few." He holds a wriggling fish up, smiling. They are surprisingly small, no more than a pound or two, but pretty and delicate. I know they taste good, I had one for dinner last night at a restaurant. "But these— too small." He tosses them overboard without a further glance. The others have pulled out plastic baskets, where Asher slides the good fish. Egrets, standing on the corks of the net, move in closer now as bodies start to fly. They know what's coming.

"Sardines," he says now, collecting about a dozen of them. "Can't sell. Not enough." He tosses them into a basket and hands it to the Danish girl, who dumps them overboard.

"These—no good," he says to me, sorting out at least a dozen spiny-looking fish. "Nobody buys these." He puts them in a blue plastic tray and hands them to the American. He upends the tray over the side.

"Okay, these, we sell. The price is not too good, but okay." He shakes his head and shrugs.

"Are those carp?" I ask, above him, pointing to the largest fish, maybe ten pounds. There are about eight of them. He nods, and sorts even these.

I am astonished at how many fish go over the side. Some are dead and they float, their white bellies not long in the water until the egrets and gulls snap them up. It's an ugly, grisly scene, this unconscious daily enactment of Jesus' parable, the "bad" fish cast out flippantly, with a glance and toss of the wrist, then snapped and torn apart by the vicious beaks of shrieking birds.

I wonder what they thought, those men, all those years ago sitting near the lake, not far from our seine boat's travels that day. I came to Israel to find Jesus in some way, and maybe it is working, because I see them there in Peter's house in Capernaum. I arrive on foot at this village on the shores of Galilee two days after my day on the seine boat and spend the afternoon wandering the town. A few vans of people got there before me, but the ancient streets feel nearly empty. The excavations reveal stone streets and rows of basalt houses, one of which is believed to be Peter's. I climb the steps of the Franciscan church built over the crumbling walls of Peter's house and look down through the glass into perhaps the very rooms Jesus ate and slept in, perhaps the very room where he had explained the parables. I stand just feet away from those rooms of dirt and rock, quivering.

What are those men doing there that day? Jesus has started a whole string of illustrations, sitting in the boat, facing that massive crowd. Each one illuminates in some way "the kingdom of heaven." First, the sower and the seed, then on to the wheat and the weeds, the mustard seed, the leaven. Does the crowd get restless, distracted? Are some arguing back or wandering away? Something happens, because halfway through Jesus stops teaching and leaves them all, but waves his men back into the house. The minute they settle in, they ask intently, "Explain the parable of the weeds in the field!" He does, and he goes on with more stories: the hidden treasure, the pearl of great price, and then the last one recorded that day, the sorting of the fish.

Even in the speaking of the parables that day, it has already begun: the sorting, the dividing. Though no one understands their deeper meaning, many of the listeners are intrigued by these simple stories from their own neighborhood. They recognize all the elements—seeds, yeast, wheat, fish—and each one ends with a surprising twist. But Yeshua is asking something of all of them, even in the listening. He asks them for "ears to hear." He asks them to combine these stories with even a mustard seed of faith, enough to come and ask him, "What does this mean?" Do any of the disciples see this then, that the parables enact their own truths even in the telling? As Jesus speaks, the crowds part, divide, parse out into those who are hungry to learn and know more about God and the Kingdom of Heaven, and those who are not. And many of them do have ears to hear, enough to cram Peter's house with men and women who have to know more. But most turn and walk away.

If you walked away, then, from this Good News of the coming of God to his people, what would happen? Yeshua's stories that day show them. The last one—the sorting of the fish—hits them hardest, especially the fishermen. Who then are the "clean" fish, the "good" fish? Is it really them? They look around at one another. There they are, a tax-taker, a revolutionary, a handful of scaly fishermen, and an assortment of others who eat with prostitutes and publicans. Some of them are despised. A few are feared. Most are ignored. What an outrageous reversal this is, that they are chosen, accepted, loved, named "clean" by this man who might be the Messiah! In Roman hands, they would all be thrown to the buzzards. Some of their own people would have judged the same. But not this man who entered their lives with open hands and invitations. They are astounded! They knew their faith is small and weak, but it is strong enough to place them by Yeshua's side.

I am astounded as well. I'm as unclean as they come—a Gentile, lost, selfish, cherishing my rebellions—yet here I stand, named "clean"! The audacity of Jesus! To love people like me, like them, and to move us toward faith in him! To sweep so many undeserving into heaven! But the others to judgment, "weeping," the "blazing furnace." I don't want to hear these words.

This parable is a double-edged sword for all of us—for me as a present-day stumbler after Christ, and for them, the first followers. All of us will be shaken. They will falter later over the "clean" fish, over the gospel's invitation to everyone, not just the Jewish people. I falter now—as a twenty-first-century American raised on "God is love"—over the "unclean" fish that will fall into judgment.

But they hear the news differently than I do. Raised in oppression, with a long history of slavery and persecution, they are likely gladdened at this sorting. *Here it comes!* they are likely thinking. *At last, our enemies will be destroyed and we will be vindicated!*

If I were there among those first followers that day, I would protest. But not to Jesus' face. Later. I'd wait until I was alone with the disciples.

Brothers, I would start. They would look at me askance, not knowing yet that this Gentile woman can indeed be part of their spiritual family. *How is this good news?* I would ask them, respectfully. *I saw you all nod at the sorting of the fish. At the burning of the weeds in the field. You just accepted it all. Don't you want all people to be saved? Why can't the Messiah just leave this last part out?*

The men would look startled at first. Then they would look at me with pity.

But it has always been so, someone would start. Who would it be? Peter, probably. He was usually the first to respond. *Don't you see? From the moment we were called, God separated us, chose us as a special people set apart for himself. He taught us to make distinctions between what was clean and unclean in everything we did: our food, our clothing, our worship. To sort out the holy from the common. We have done this all our lives. As a fisherman, I can tell you, the fish must be sorted!*

Andrew bursts in. *We had a choice right from the beginning of all this! Did you hear what John called out from the river? "Repent! Turn the other way!" To turn toward this Kingdom means turning away from the other. Did you see how many people walked away from Yeshua today? They don't want to listen to him or follow him.*

John steps forward now. John the fisherman. John the beloved, who wrote his own account of his time with Jesus. His face is tender as he speaks to me. *Look at our history. God set us apart, and we do it too. All people do. We divide ourselves by our own choices: Are we going to follow God, or not? Are we going to obey God, or not? Are we going to build our lives around God or around ourselves? We make the choice first. God will honor the choices we make. He sorts us by the choices we have made.*

I am listening to them intently, but my face shows uncertainty. Peter turns to me again, eyes fiery, looking deeply into mine. *If there is no sorting, if there is no difference in the end in how you live and who you follow and who you obey, then this life doesn't matter.* He pauses for effect. *Then there is no justice, no setting aright this crooked world. There is no message of Good News. Not for anyone.*

I notice, all the men who have spoken to me are fishermen. They know even more than the others how real and how necessary the sorting is. They nod their heads at me and turn back to find Jesus. I would turn away, back to my own time, to my own beach, to the nets still waiting to be mended. And I see it suddenly in the nets in my own hands. Before this net can be mended and whole again, the edges must be squared. All the tattered and trailing pieces must be cut out first. It's impossible to sew new webbing into shredded holes. I see it. Judgment must come, the final end to oppression, self-centeredness, and every form of destruction before it can begin, the full rule of the Messiah over his creation and his people. All cannot be restored and renewed without it. With our selfish choices, we rend the world; God's judgment will mend the world.

But my brothers are not right about all of it. Not the "coming soon" part. They would never have imagined that followers of Jesus are still waiting two thousand years later. Yes, death has been vanquished, but oppression has not.

I know what is coming next for those men. Yeshua himself will go to the cross to kill death, and he will rise again, so that his people will rise again. Sin and death will be defeated, heaven will be open to all who repent, the Kingdom of God has begun, but here we are still. Here I am standing at the shredded nets, quaking with the reality of broken families, sufferings, and persecutions around the world. It's not over yet.

There is a final judgment coming. Because I thirst for peace and hunger for restoration, I long for it. I long for the repair of this world.

I stand here sorting and mending, my needle moving once, twice, three times around and cinching into a knot so tight, I hope the ocean and fish and seals cannot pull it out. I want to mend the houses and homes of the Syrians bombed, I want to sew up the holes in their hearts for their mother, their grandfather, their brothers killed in the war. I want to sew up the holes in my own heart for my own family.

As the hole cinches, as the absence, needle-stroke by needle-stroke, is filled in, as I graft in the other webbing, the old into the new, my spinning, knotting hands speak to me as well. I see my own part in all of this, my own bent toward selfishness and destruction. I am guarding my heart, nursing my wounds, holding on bloody-fisted to my rights, turning away from those I love most. I am causing rupture and division.

I recognize now the power of the gospel. I do not have to wait for the final sorting and the judgment to make it right. I cannot change the wars in the Middle East, I cannot reconcile racial tensions around the world, but I can do this: I can turn from my anger. I can love. I can forgive.

I am on the last side of another patch I am sewing. It is evening now. When I am done, I will put down my needle and scissors, walk up that long hill to my house and write a letter to my family, a letter of love and reconciliation. And one more thing. I look over at Duncan, who is concentrating on a hole, his brow furrowed. Duncan, who works so hard for all of us. I stand up straight, look at him in the eyes until he sees me. I smile and blink my eyes. He watches me for a moment, then smiles and blinks back. We nod, looking at each other for a few seconds, then we laugh and turn back to the last meshes in our hands.

This net is almost mended.

CHAPTER EIGHT

STORMING THE PEACE

That day when evening came, he said to his disciples, "Let us go over to the other side." Leaving the crowd behind, they took him along, just as he was, in the boat. There were also other boats with him. A furious squall came up, and the waves broke over the boat, so that it was nearly swamped. Jesus was in the stern, sleeping on a cushion. The disciples woke him and said to him, "Teacher, don't you care if we drown?"

He got up, rebuked the wind and said to the waves, "Quiet! Be still!" Then the wind died down and it was completely calm.

He said to his disciples, "Why are you so afraid? Do you still have no faith?"

They were terrified and asked each other, "Who is this? Even the wind and the waves obey him!"

MARK 4:35-41

DUNCAN AND I ARE GOING on a date. It's hard to do when you live with ten others on a roadless island in the Alaskan bush. But we've learned to snag any moment alone, no matter what we're doing, and call it a date. Here it is! A trip to Larsen Bay! The nets were mended and set back in the water two days ago. We're taking some visiting friends to the gravel airstrip in Larsen Bay. We wave good-bye and leave the sheltered beach, rounding the corner into the bay. We look at each other suddenly and smile—alone! I sidle up close to Duncan for a snuggle in our thick rain gear, but our surprise and joy is short lived. It was already blowing southeast when we left the island, but the wind is picking up by the minute. Within five minutes of leaving the harbor, the water is already a dark tempest, the tops white with foam. Forget the date. It's time to hold on, to watch each wave to see how it will break, to brace our bodies as the skiff drop-slams into every falling wave.

Halfway through our bumpy slog home, the engine slows, then coughs, and before we know it, we are dead in the water. Duncan bends to pump the gas bulb, then turns the ignition. Nothing. I check the gas tank to make sure it isn't air locked. It's not. The problem is even more basic: We're out of gas. In our hurry not to miss the plane, we forgot to check all the gas tanks in the skiff to make sure they were full. We stand there looking at each other in disbelief. But we can't stand incredulous for too long: It's blowing twenty-five knots onshore, pushing us toward cliff and beach. We know this could go badly. We yank the oars out of their ties on the railings and discover the paddle ends are cracked and half broken. They'll have to do. Now it's just our arms and these broken paddles against the wind and a raging tide and current that's already blowing us to a wave-shattering shore. All it takes is one little oversight, and we are in danger.

I know the Gospels record some troubles and danger for the fishermen and disciples on the Sea of Galilee, but while there I find it hard to believe. For two weeks, I walk beside still waters, go out with fishermen on calm seas, watch the sun rise and set on a halcyon lake. It seems only a faraway fairy tale, the watery, dramatic story that comes next in the Gospels. I pray for days, "Lord, show me a storm." It is mid-November, and I've happened to hit a heat wave: It has been eighty-five degrees nearly every day, the heat causing a veil of haze and fog over the water and surrounding hills. I cannot in my highest, most faith-inspired imagination envision a boat full of fishermen believing they were about to drown in these tepid waters. The next part of the story is hard enough to believe—speaking the storm to sudden peace? But I cannot even get there without a storm.

Lord, show me a storm.

I had read about the summer squalls that descend upon the lake. An elderly man who runs the House of Anchors, a tiny one-room museum of ancient fishing implements in Ein Gev, told me about the storms, how they come in summer, sweeping down out of the hills, whipping the water into froth. Asher, the seine fisherman I went out with that day, told me too, that the storms come suddenly. The moment they see them coming, sweeping down from the hills, though they are in a thirty-two-foot boat, they pull up their nets, rev up the engines, and nose back into the harbor. No one stays out when the waters go white.

The last few days in Tiberias, I was walking the promenade

for my tenth time one Thursday morning when I felt it: wind. The palm trees above me rustled nervously. The waters stirred. My heart stirred with it. I stayed for the next few hours, watching the wind rise, observing the quiet waters lifting higher and higher to whitecaps until the fleet of boats with names like *Faith*, *Hope*, *Joy* elbowed their slips, bumping the docks. It wasn't long until the lake surged and broke against the seawall, showering the entire promenade with a rhythmic whoosh every half minute or so.

The usual strolling crowd disappeared. I was nearly alone now, face into the wind, shielding my eyes as I looked out over the equally deserted waters. I smiled. Yes, a boat could sink out there. A boat without an engine, even a boat like the Jesus boat I had seen at Ginosar, unearthed in 1986, a boat dated to Jesus' time. It was much bigger than I had imagined fishing boats to be on the Galilee—thirty feet. But fill it full of men, stir up the sea, give them only muscle-powered oars and no life jackets and no Coast Guard to rescue them and yes, they might drown, all of them. A storm! Glory, I can believe in this part of the story at least!

I've been in many storms on the water. Early one April, I was lost in a snowstorm on the ocean in a tiny wooden boat half the size of the kind these men were in. I was twenty-three. I was traveling from a herring cannery Duncan and I were working in out to our island, a ten-mile journey across empty waters and vacant shorelines. Only a handful of people live out in the bush around Kodiak through the winter. I was halfway to the island when the squall hit. The heavy spring snow instantly erased both land and seascape until I could see nothing but a small patch of water before me. I was disoriented. Where do I go? My stomach tightened as I motored slowly, blindly in the snow. If I wasn't careful, I would end up in the Shelikof Strait, that two-hundred-mile-long by fifty-mile-wide tunnel of stormy waters where too many boats had gone down. My tiny skiff had no business in the Shelikof, especially in April, as cold and blowing as any winter month. I had to find land. I motored slowly through the snow, eyes willing any piece of land into sight until I saw it—a cliffed shoreline on my right. Land ho!

I was immediately relieved, until I realized I didn't recognize this high-rocked cliff. Where was I? But I wasn't worried. I would follow it and soon I'd hit a beach or an island, something I knew. And I'd be at my island soon after. On I went in the heavy snow, one hand over my eyes. I was glad I had worn my winter down coat and thick mittens. Time flurried by, and cliff after cliff passed, while I strained to recognize a promontory, a rock outcropping, but nothing looked familiar. I wondered if I had somehow ended up in Norway, so strange did it all appear in the snow.

Somewhere along the way, the engine, an old Johnson 35, began to cough and sputter. I throttled down, and it died. I didn't panic. I yanked the pull cord to start it again. Nothing. Again. Nothing. I looked around with growing fear. I was dead in the water with nowhere to go. But the water was anything but dead. Wind and wave pushed me toward the cliffs I had been following. I knew I had to start the engine, and I had to start it now. I gave one final pull with all my might—and it broke. The cord, now half its length, hung useless in my hand.

Now I had only what those twelve men had in their storm—oars to move my wooden boat. Stricken, knowing I had to row fast to stay out of the surge against the cliffs, I fumbled to find the oarlocks. I set them in place while watching the waves, then pulled the heavy oars out from the rails, then awkwardly set them in the oarlocks. They were heavy. I began rowing, but badly. I had to sync my arms, grip the right place on the oars, get the right end positioned in the water for the best pull. I rowed pathetically at first, as if both these oars were crutches and I couldn't make them work right. I didn't have the right muscles. And the skiff, small though it was, was old and lumbering, made of planks.

So I know this just a little, how hard it is to power a thick wooden boat against a rough sea with nothing but arms, with all the elements piling up against me: the blinding snow, the unfamiliar terrain, the surging waters against the cliff. How long until the waves flung me against the cliff and the boat smashed and I was in the water, with just minutes to live? I know that helplessness, that wild panic.

It's not hard, then, for me to see them there in the middle of the lake, all available hands on all the oars, in waves now breaking over the boat's sides and stern. Mark's Gospel says the water was filling the boat.[1] Matthew's says the waves were sweeping over the boat.[2] The waves did not breach my little wooden boat that April day, but other times—so many other times—the waves have indeed swept over and into our boat until suddenly we are sitting in water up to the calves of our boots. The skipper, Duncan, or any one of us yell at the others, "Start bailing!" and we grab the five-gallon bucket behind us. Pitching with the boat and the seas, we bend and scoop the water back as fast as we can while lashed by rain and spray. Or the order given is simply, "Let's get out of here!" and we let go of the net and rev the sixty-horse outboard, rising up out of those twisting, malicious seas, headed for harbor and calm, knowing just two more of those waves could sink us.

So I am there with them in this boat as they cross. I can see their muscles bulging as they beat their oars against the furious sea, these harsh short waves with a wicked chop. They are shouting at one another, "Bartholemew—bail!" "Pull harder, John!" "Swing the bow around, Andrew!" There are too many in the boat, and the waves are too rough. They cannot keep a forward momentum, the boat falls between troughs, and soon just a few more waves will swamp them entirely.

They didn't see this storm coming. They were in Capernaum, at Peter's house, where Jesus lived as well. That afternoon, Jesus healed Peter's mother-in-law of a fever. By evening, the whole town knew. They gathered their sick, infirm, and demon-oppressed and stood pleading, hopeful at Peter's door. Jesus healed them all. Every one. People kept coming until a crowd massed around him, and Jesus knew it was time to go. He wanted to cross to the eastern side. They could walk, but the crowds would follow, and their boats were already there. No one was thinking about the weather. And if anyone saw the brewing storm before they stepped into the boat, they surely thought, *Jesus is with us. What could happen?*

All is well the first mile. The men are talking as they sail and row together, but in lower tones. Jesus is exhausted and tells them he's going to rest. He finds a cushion in the stern, stretches out, and is already gone. He has put himself under their power entirely. He is always the one in front, in charge, knowing where to go and how to get there. This time, he has entrusted himself to them, these men of the sea. He is so depleted from a night of healings, nothing wakes him. Not the pitching of the boat, the rain, the waves sweeping over, the men's grunts and shouts as they row for their very lives.

I know what some of them are thinking! It's all a mess, this night. The storm is bad enough, but their confusion is worse. Andrew maybe feels deeply confused and hurt. Their teacher just saved and healed all the ill and deformed; he's rescued all the dying, but what about them? He remembers his words from the long teaching on the hillside that day, about the lilies, the sparrows, how much God cares for them; they are not to worry about their life. They cannot add one moment to their lives by worrying. How can this be true? Are they not to care that they are sinking? They have no way to stay afloat in such waters . . . they all know they could drown. Drowning is their lifelong fear, these men who work on the water, all of whom have lost friends and family to the wild, blowing sea. This whole enterprise, following this man Jesus, is a total bust then, if it all ends here. All of them wiped out at once.

The water is past their ankles as they row. And there he lies! Sleeping like a child with no responsibilities at all. How can he be with them, and yet unconscious of them? At every lash of spray, they look at his reclining form incredulously. Their faith—their early, young faith—is shaken to the core. Their rabbi has just showed again his power over demons and disease, but now he is overpowered by sleep? How can he cure the dying but not keep himself awake?

They need him. They need him to take a turn at the oars. They need him to at least give them extra strength. And there is one last outrage. Look, Jesus is not just knocked out and not helping: He is lying on the one object that could help them— the sea anchor! Mark gives us this detail, that he is asleep on a "cushion."[3] Mendel Nun, the expert on biblical fishing on the Sea of Galilee, tells us this is likely the buoy for the sea anchor, the anchor that was dropped to give a struggling boat some stability in rough seas.

It is even worse, then. Jesus is not only oblivious to their dire straits, but this carpenter has co-opted their only chance to ride out the storm. The fishermen must be angry, if they can feel anger while yet fearing for their very lives.

Their doubt rises as high as the seas. He's asleep. He's just a man, after all. He can't save them from the storm. He can't even wake up. Whatever they thought about Jesus, whatever they learned—they give it up now. They were wrong. His powers are limited. His love is limited. He is all too human.

The wind keens yet higher, and they argue now over waking him. Some are afraid to wake him; others wanted to wake him at the very start of the blow. But now, another wave has swept over the side, the water is up to their calves, and no one asks anymore. They're about to die. Jesus is their last resort.

The ones not on the oars stumble back and nearly fall on him. His robes are as plastered to his body as theirs, yet still he sleeps. One puts his hand on Jesus' shoulder and shakes him. "Master, don't you care that we're drowning?" *Don't you care?* They assume he knows. They do not assume he cares. Despite all that Jesus has done for them, despite his unrelenting love toward them, and the intimate daily relationship he has called them into, they doubt his love.

That moment came for me as well. I did not believe that I would drown, but I did not know how I would survive that day. I wondered if God knew, if he saw, if he truly loved me after all. I had oars, but I had nowhere to go. Where I had come, motoring slowly and carefully, there were only cliffs, not a single beach to safely land my skiff on. Standing in the falling snow, with oars in my hands and nowhere to go, I had nothing left. I did what they finally did: "Lord! Where are you? Don't you care? Help me!" I aimed at the smothering clouds above.

We know what happens next in that first story, how impossible it all is, that an entire world of storm is settled with three words. That one man can wake up, then stand up in a wild-horse boat on a stampeding sea and in the moment he speaks—*Peace! Be still!*—the seas lie down to sleep. The wind holds its breath. From hurricane to hush. Three words. Not a breath. Not a whisper. The men, lashed and soaked, with the oars still in their hands, are panting, as if the cessation of wind has sucked out their own. They tremble as they gape at him standing there. They are safe now, they know.

It happened almost like this in my own story. In that instant, yes, *in that instant* that I hurled my prayer north, the snow stopped for the first time that afternoon, the clouds parted, and I could finally see. I saw the one thing I needed above all else: a beach. I could see a beach across the arm of the bay. One small beach that I could row to and land the skiff on. I was not saved yet, but I would be safe soon, at least from the ocean and the storm. With much effort, I rowed over to that beach, the one beach visible and reachable, and hunkered down under a cottonwood tree, grateful for a desperate prayer answered, for the earth beneath me.

That night, after feeding the fire I had built that afternoon one more time, I settled in for the night under a tarp I had rigged up, tied to two nearby trees. It was 8:30 p.m. Completely dark. My main concern was bears—I knew they were wandering out of their dens already—and keeping the fire going, not only for warmth, but for a signal. Impossibly, not long after I took up my resigned post, I heard a plane. Who would be flying in the dark? I scrambled to my feet and did what I had done all day every time a plane had come near: I threw gas from a bucket onto the flame. This time, in the dark, the leap of the flames caught the pilot's eye. My ordeal was over.

I was saved that day. I was soon safe back at the cannery. But neither story is done. Because the twelve men are more terrified now in the calm than they were in the tempest. They know how quickly storm and horror can strike. But peace like milk, water like silk in a second because a man spoke? Storms take days to swell out and die. Now they are truly terrified. Now "they feared with great fear."[4]

And Jesus is not pleased with them. In Mark's Gospel, he rebukes them now, after the stilling of the gale. "Why are you so afraid? Have you *still* no faith?"[5]

Have you still *no faith even after what I've shown you, what I've done for you?* But they are too confused and afraid to believe. Afraid that this man might be who he seemed to be.

They have seen his mastery over the creatures they have spent their lives learning to catch. Disease obeys and abandons bodies, demons flee at his touch and word. Even when he started, "his disciples put their faith in him"[6] at the wedding when he turned water in a jug to wine. But no man can touch the wide blue sea. No man can shout down the wind. Is he a man, then, this one? John called him "the Lamb of God, who takes away the sin of the world!"[7] What lamb can stop the roar of the wind and sea?

This story ends with a question spoken from the hurricane of fear in their hearts: "Who then is this, that even the wind and the sea obey him?"[8]

But it's not really over. I live in a place (don't we all?) where storms come one on the heels of another. And Jesus doesn't rescue everyone from the raging gales. Sinners, saints, they've all gone down in equal measure. That is hard enough. But there is more. What if the waters are calm, and people drown anyway? What then? What do we believe then? I ask, because this day in the middle of the salmon season I am leaving Harvester Island and going out fishing on a seine boat with a man who lost everything one day right here in the same bay where I was lost and found.

We ran into Dave the night before, in the lagoon. He was anchored up there, his forty-eight-foot boat *The Dreamer* sitting lazily at rest in the night sun. He knew I wanted to go seining with him someday. "Hey Leslie, you wanna go out with me tomorrow?" he asked, leaning his head out the window. His shoulder-length hair is streaked with grey, his face chiseled from nearly seventy years on the ocean. He knows I've always wanted to go out on a seine boat and see how other fishermen live and work. All I know is setnetting. It's lost its charm. I want to fall in love with fishing again, and maybe I can.

The next morning at six, Dave's seine skiff noses into our beach. I am ready, waiting with a small backpack of gear for the day. His crewman, Frank, nods at me without smiling. I nod back. I step out into the water, vault noisily over the side of the skiff. The wind is still today, I notice. Not a breath, just light fog wisping about the grey waters. I am nervous leaving my island for the day. I step onto the rail. Dave extends his massive hand. He pulls and I leap, landing on deck.

"Glad you're here today, " Dave says solemnly. I look past his enormous bushy eyebrows to his one good eye. "It's a big day. This is the anniversary, today. It's been forty years."

I am stricken, almost panicked as I keep my eyes on his. He is calm and steady, but I am not. I did not know this was the day.

What will I do on such a day? What will I say? I will not ask him what happened, I decide instantly. I will talk about it only if he wants to. I've known the story since I arrived here thirty-eight years ago. It does not take long to tell. Dave was winter watchman at a remote cannery fourteen miles from our island. He spent many winters there, taking care of the cluster of ware-houses and buildings that sit on stilts between mountain and ocean, deep in the veins of Uyak Bay. His father, seventy-one, was living there with him that winter. He was a Jesus follower who lived as a missionary out on faraway Unga Island in the Aleutians in a village of a hundred people. He wasn't sponsored by any mission agency. He was going it alone, loving the people just as they were, Dave once told me.

Dave's son, Skeeter, was excited his grandfather was there. His grandfather was enormously strong and had hunted bear and seal and lived the life of a frontiersman. There were so many stories to be told! And likely he was telling one that day the two of them set out from the cannery in a skiff to go hunt-ing. It was a special day. It was Skeeter's fourteenth birthday. They took one of the dogs, a black lab, and two rifles. It was a calm day. Just a little wind chop on the water. Nothing to even pay attention to. One of those days you feel like a water strider, skimming perfectly across the water. Hours passed and they did not return. Dave, concerned, went out to look for them. Others from Larsen Bay came out as well. They found the skiff drifting, with the dog and the rifle still in it, and nothing else. They were gone. They had slipped beneath those quiet black waters, waters without a hint of storm or danger that day. Had Skeeter fallen out and his grandfather then jumped in to save him?

Dave needed to know. He had a theory: The skiff they were using was a derelict skiff Skeeter had rebuilt over the winter. That morning they went hunting had been its first launch. Dave took it out on the same waters, with the same light wind. The bow hit a little six-inch chop and sheared so hard it would have thrown Dave out of the boat, except he had wrapped his legs around the seat. He knew now what happened.

On this same day, forty years later, Dave and his partner, Renee, and their two crew catch a lot of fish. I am there with them, stacking corks on deck, eating dinner at the table. Dave and I sit together in the wheelhouse on the skipper's throne and talk about God, about why bad things happen. "I don't know why I lost my son. I'd been looking forward to having a son since I was twelve years old," Dave says calmly with his resonant voice. "I have a friend who says it was Satan. Who says every bad thing that happens is from Satan. I don't believe that." Then in a quieter voice he says, "I found my dad's body the next day. Where we found their skiff, drifting, down there close to the cannery, there's a patch of forget-me-nots that bloom on the beach every year. There, just there and nowhere else in that area. That's a holy place," he says, as I close my eyes for the tears. We are silent in the wonder and fear of it.

Before I said yes to Duncan, that I would marry him and make this island and its waters my home, this was one of the very first stories Duncan told me. He wanted me to know that this place was dangerous. That people could die here, just like that. Just by falling out of a boat on a calm day. He wanted me to know that living here had a cost. Duncan was right.

But no one warned me about the Christian life, that pledging my whole self to this Jesus would not change my world. That life would still be dangerous. That my new faith would not end the shaking of my childhood rooms, would not take away the poverty, the fights, the despair that lived in our house.

I am not done with questions. There are so many storms in life. What about the storm of fire? Can we trust him through the pain and loss and storm of fire? Because there was a fire. It started in the kitchen in the early hours of the morning, long before anyone was up. But one person, up in the night, saw the house aflame. And my mother-in-law, Wanda, was inside. I wasn't there, but others were: her eldest son, a handful of crewmen, her youngest son a mile away. They broke the window to get in. One climbed inside, keeping low to the ground. He could not see for the smoke. He could not find her, and he could not breathe. He fell back out of the window, heaving. He tried again in a moment, after his breath came back. He could not find her again, and now he might die too; the flames were closer, and no air was left to breathe. He fell out for the last time, and the house was nearly gone.

I was in Kodiak, sleeping. The alarm was set to get up early to finish packing to leave. We would soon be flying out to join Wanda and Duncan's brothers and crew for another fishing season. In my sleep, I heard someone pounding on our bedroom door. I jumped up, panicked, to open it. It was my sister-in-law. "Wanda's house burned down. She's gone." And the shock and tears that wouldn't stop.

She was a follower of Jesus. She had loved and served him her whole life, without pause or question. Church organist, church everything, generous, always thoughtful. She loved her life out at Bear Island. She loved the wildflowers, the beaches. What peace could be spoken into this storm?

From the start, I knew Jesus as a rescuing God who saved me from myself, from my lonely and loveless life, from my own proud and self-sufficient heart. And I have seen so much more. He parted the clouds for me that day, tamed the sea and stopped the snow to show me a beach. He sent a neighbor to tow us home that day Duncan and I ran out of gas in the southeast blow. I believe he is with us in every storm, but how many boats have gone down just in this corner of the sea? How many men and women lost when the flames were not quenched, when the waters were not calmed? Yes, so many saved, but so many lost. Even those who knew Jesus. I know he told it straight and often, "Whoever wants to be my disciple must deny themselves and take up their cross and follow me."[9] I know that "take up their cross" means to be ready to die. But who can do this?

Now I am with the men panting on the floor of the boat, soaked and shaking. Because we know the truth now. That Jesus, this God-man, can command every element of creation with just a word, but he does not always take away the winds. Jesus can sit in a boat with us, and that boat still might sink. Is there then no easy heaven here in this dangerous world? Even for us, his chosen ones, his followers? If we who follow after him cannot even be sure he will save us, how can we trust him?

What kind of Savior will you be to us, Jesus? Will you save us from the storm? More, Jesus, will you save us from you? You who calm the storm—are the storm most of all, Jesus. Would you save us from ourselves, because our faith is so small and our fear is so great?

I have seen the thatch of wild grasses that grow where Wanda's house once stood. I skiff down there sometimes, to her island, just a mile from ours. I sit on the lone rock wall where the porch used to be, over the grasses and wildflowers she loved, growing now from the ashes. I tremble.

Peace, be still?

CHAPTER NINE

FILLING
THE HUNGRY

When Jesus heard what had happened, he withdrew by boat privately to a solitary place. Hearing of this, the crowds followed him on foot from the towns. When Jesus landed and saw a large crowd, he had compassion on them and healed their sick.

As evening approached, the disciples came to him and said, "This is a remote place, and it's already getting late. Send the crowds away, so they can go to the villages and buy themselves some food."

Jesus replied, "They do not need to go away. You give them something to eat."

"We have here only five loaves of bread and two fish," they answered.

"Bring them here to me," he said. And he directed the people to sit down on the grass. Taking the five loaves and the two fish and looking up to heaven, he gave thanks and broke the loaves. Then he gave them to the disciples, and the disciples gave them to the people. They all ate and were satisfied, and the disciples picked up twelve basketfuls of broken pieces that were left over. The number of those who ate was about five thousand men, besides women and children.

MATTHEW 14:13-21

THE BREAD DOUGH FEELS GOOD under my hands, fleshy and supple as a body. I'm almost done kneading. This should make ten loaves of whole grain baguettes. I've just finished two batches of salmonberry jam to add to the chest-high stack of cases in the attic. The kitchen is a disaster, as usual. Kristi is here with me, finishing lunch. In just twenty minutes the fishermen will be in from the nets. Nine people will fill the doorway and drop to their seats, famished, knowing they'll be fed well.

It's the third week in July now. I've not been out on the water at all this last week, spending most of my days and nights immersed in fish, words, and meals. A book must be written, ten people must be fed, the freezers must be filled for the winter. The skiff is my occasional escape now. I find myself longing to launch out onto the water, responsible for one thing alone: get the fish out of the nets.

Just as I start setting the table, I hear the ATV roaring up to the house and the excited feet of news on the doorstep.

"Mom! You gotta come! Isaac and I got a huge halibut!"

"Really?" I say, meeting Micah on the porch.

"Everyone's down on the beach!"

I jump down the steps after Micah. We haven't had fresh halibut for a while.

Halibut are ugly, but they're magical, too. They're flat fish that feed on the bottom, and swim flat like a stingray, moving like a wave. They can grow as huge as five hundred pounds. One side, the side with both eyes on top, is mottled green and black, perfect camouflage for the bottom, where they lie waiting for unsuspecting prey. The other side is white as the moon. The flesh is flaky and sweet.

Micah leaps onto the ATV. I climb on behind him, letting him drive. We bump and twist over the grassy lumps, then hit the beach, where everyone is standing around the tractor and the prize hanging from it: a halibut that's bigger than me. The crew are grinning; Isaac is telling the story again, how he was out jigging and then felt an enormous yank. He pulled it up, this massive load of white he wasn't even sure was a fish. Maybe it was a shark. But then somehow it got free and was just fluttering near the surface, dazed. He reached out and grabbed the tail, and with Micah's help put a line around it. They knew they couldn't lift it in by themselves, so they just tied the line onto the skiff and waited for help. Twenty minutes later one of the fishing skiffs came by, and one of the crew jumped in to help. Then another. It took four of them to slide the giant fish into the boat.

"It's over a hundred pounds for sure. What do you think, Dad?" Isaac asks.

Duncan's on the tractor now, lifting the halibut so its nose hangs just inches from the ground.

"Yeah, I'd say maybe bigger, like a hundred and fifty pounds. We can measure it from nose to tail, and then we can find out what it weighs. I'll drive it up to the house, then go check."

With everyone standing in their orange rain gear, red bandanas, hats, the beach is alive with color and bodies and happy faces. Everyone wants to stand next to the behemoth and claim it as their own. Isaac lifts Micah up to hang from the forklift next to the halibut. I am there with my camera. Snap. Then all the boys gather around the fish with giant grins and manly arm poses. Snap. We are all delighted that the morning and the ocean delivered something so wondrous to our hands.

Even the word *halibut* is wondrous to me. It comes from *haly*, the Old English word for holy, and *butt*, which referred to any fish that fed on the bottom. The massive halibut, and other delectable butt, like turbot and sole, were traditionally saved for the holiest feast days of the church: Pascha and Christmas. This fish hanging from our tractor is nothing less than a "holy bottom fish."

Duncan revs the tractor, and the party moves slowly behind it as it grinds from the beach up to the house, where we will fillet it. As we gather and sharpen the knives, Duncan comes out to the steps, smiling, with an announcement. "Okay, everyone. I looked it up. A halibut that's six-two weighs, on average, two hundred and fifteen pounds."

"Dang!"

"For real?"

"I knew it was bigger than a hundred and fifty pounds!"

We gape anew, and then we begin to cut. For the next three hours, we are wrist deep in fish flesh, filleting the meat from the bones, then dropping the massive chunks into a bin, then carrying the bins into the kitchen, where the meat is then cut from the skin into serving-sized chunks. We pack it into bags, vacuum seal each bag, then label and stack the bags in the freezer. We don't waste anything. We get carried away and cut even the meat and skin from between the ribs. I decide I will make deep-fried halibut for the ten of us tonight, and for tomorrow, from the scraps, halibut enchiladas.

In the midst of this bounty I remember how much of this fish is lost. The halibut stocks have sharply fallen in the Gulf of Alaska the last few years. Too many large boats haul in halibut as incidental catch while fishing for other species.

Thousands of tons of beautiful white flesh are thrown overboard. Wasted.

The day after I fished with Asher, I set out for Tabgha, to the hillside where most believe the first miraculous feeding happened.
I am anxious to get there. This is one of my favorite events in
the Scriptures. Besides the Resurrection, it's the only miraculous
event included in all four Gospels. But I am beat. It is almost
ninety degrees. I am carrying a backpack and a front pack and
am soaked with sweat. I have only three more miles to go before
I can stop for the day, but I am enjoying the scenery of papyrus
reeds, date palms, and oaks. Around this northern half of the
lake, thankfully, there is little development. Most of the sites
where biblical events occurred have been conserved.

I have given up on the trail, which kept disappearing into
thickets of bamboo and bogs. Instead, I'm walking on a make-
shift path beside the highway that circumnavigates the lake.
There is little traffic today. I didn't eat much for breakfast, and
now in this heat, I am craving something cold and bubbly.
Three hours in, I see a building sitting kitty-corner that might
be a restaurant. There's no sign. It looks empty, not a car in the
tiny parking lot. I am imagining an ice-cold Diet Coke. It feels
so extravagant and indulgent to even want that. But I decide
to give it a shot.

I walk in hesitantly—it *is* a restaurant! Modest tables, chairs.
But empty. A sixtyish man with black hair suddenly appears
behind the counter. He looks at me in surprise. I walk up to
the counter.

"Do you have Diet Coke?"

"Yah, sure!" He retrieves one from the refrigerator case.

Hands it to me looking askance. "Where are you from? Are you alone?" he says in a booming voice.

"Yes, I'm traveling alone. I'm from Alaska."

"Alaska? Where are you going?" he asks, puzzled, looking at my backpack.

"I'm walking around the Kinneret."

"Ohhhhh!!" He smiles a big smile. "That is good! That is healthy! That's the best way to see our country." He looks me up and down and pronounces, "Strong woman! Ah, to be young again!"

"Oh, I am not young. I am fifty-six, and I have six children." I have been saying this at the slightest provocation from men. It's my safety shield. I want them to see me as what I am—a middle-aged mother of many.

"No!" he exclaims, shaking his head. "So many children! And you are how old?" And before I can answer, he is talking about the new coffee grinder he got from Paris and he's going to give me a cup of espresso in just a moment. I don't want any espresso, but I have a feeling he won't let me off. So begins my time with Danny.

We made it past the espresso (I did have to drink it) and are on to grinding sesame seeds for tahini when a man walks in. White hair, a white T-shirt, and wild multicolored pajama pants. He looks about sixty as well.

"It's a ****** beautiful day, isn't it! Hey, who are you? I'm Jack." He speaks with a British accent and a familiarity with expletives. He holds out his hand and grabs mine with vigor.

"I'm Leslie. "

And it begins all over again. Who I am. What I'm doing here. I discover that Danny and Jack are good friends.

"You're both going to eat lunch with me," Danny announces. "Leslie, come back here in the kitchen and help me cook."

Everything he has said to me since I arrived forty-five minutes ago has been a command. I have nothing better to do this noontime, so I obey. I dig in my backpack for a shirt to put over my sweat-drenched tank top and go through the swinging doors to the kitchen.

"Put olives and salad on a plate." He gestures to a shelf of plates, and I think I know where the salads are. I reach for the plates—"No, no," he scolds. "Not those!" He points somewhere I cannot see. I take a risk and pull out flat plates. Then I go to where the salads are in a glass case and put some olives on a plate. "No, not like that. Here, olives on these," he chides, and he hands me little plates.

I have no idea what he wants or is thinking for this meal. Or what this meal is, actually. It seems I'm doing it right finally. He nods. I put the dishes on the table, clear my front pack. He brings more plates. I put silverware on, and soon he brings out three dishes of shakshuka, poached eggs in a spicy tomato and onion sauce. I know it's often served for breakfast in Israel and apparently for lunch as well.

It is all on the table now, a veritable feast—the table bright with carrots, the shakshuka, dates, crimson tomatoes, and black olives. There is mint tea as well, served in tall glasses. We eat slowly and yet hungrily, each of us. And we talk. We talk of many things: Alaska, Israel, our children. Daniel has three children, a son who is a doctor, another a chemist, all successful. Jack has two children, and grandchildren as well. We talk about them, what they're doing. They ask about my children. I give them thumbnails of each. We talk about God. Jack tells me of his conversion, how he came to believe in a god of synchronicity, who blesses him, but who requires nothing of him.

"I like this god. He blesses me all the time. I know he's with me. And he asks nothing back from me!" he says, triumphantly. Jack speaks loudly with wild hand gestures, using curses and crudities liberally to further emphasize his opinions.

They ask about my hike and what I'm doing. I tell them about this book, that I'm here to learn more about Jesus. They do not flinch but look at me curiously.

Soon another man comes in, David, who is a farmer. He brings in his dog, a Jack Russell terrier, whom Danny says is a person. David sits down to join us, and now we are four. He is just back from Cuba, where he has been teaching farmers a new irrigation system.

Another hour passes. When I finally leave, Jack offers to drive me wherever I want to go. Danny offers me a free room in his hostel behind the restaurant. Yesterday, as I left the boat, Asher insisted on giving me five of their biggest fish. Just a few miles from Tabgha, hillside of the feast, I've been fed to overflowing.

I arrive at the hillside an hour later in peace, heart open from so much generosity. I am relieved to find there is no one and nothing here. I am alone. The wind is blowing lightly, the sun is warm, the grass is spiky and thin, the ground dry beneath my feet as I climb the gentle slope, slowly, imagining the scene two thousand years ago. The disciples' arrival could not have been more different from mine. They are fleeing Capernaum, in turmoil. Yeshua's cousin, the man who brought them to the Christ, the man standing in the river, shouting, unafraid, who was the first to say, "There, the Lamb of God!" is dead: his head axed from his body at the drunken whim of Herod, who was swayed by a girl's dance. The first shouts of the coming of heaven now silenced. The men are crushed, grieving. They have buried his mangled body themselves.

Since they joined Jesus months before, they have come to see that he speaks both peace and storm, and now they know the storm bears a sword. He has said it before, "I have come to bring a sword to the earth," but they thought something different, all of them, especially Simon the Zealous One, who saw it as Rome crushed beneath their own raised sword, Yeshua leading the charge. Nothing like this has happened. And now the sword has come down on their necks. On *his* neck. How can this be? Why didn't Yeshua save him? They remember him sleeping in the boat while they were nearly sinking. They are shaken to their core.

In the boat, no one speaks as they sail. They long for this quiet on the water. Soon they will climb a remote hill and find out what his death will mean to them, what they will do. But when they arrive, when the boat touches the sandy shore, their faces freeze. The hillside, this empty place far from any village, is alive with bodies. And more people are still coming by foot even then, running. Others were already there, sitting, waiting. Waiting for him, they know.

They turn to him. What will he do? Weary with grief, Jesus lifts his head, breathes deeply, looks upon the thousands, steps out of the boat, and immediately lays hands on a girl who cannot walk, carried by her mother straight to him. There he is, Yeshua, giving it all away—again. All day long. Maybe the men see what it means to carry the news of the Kingdom of God: that you will give up even your mourning for those who need to hear it, and your dinner, and anything else you thought might have been yours.

At the end of that day, this day when they have watched what they have seen so many times before—the crooked bodies straight, the invalids on their feet, the silent laughing praises—there is yet one more need. One more need for all of them. They are hungry. Jesus, too. He has healed every body—and every healed body needs food.

We know what happens with this lunch of five barley loaves and two salted sardines, the crust and flesh splitting, dividing in Jesus' hands, filling every outstretched hand, every mouth, every appetite. The families and neighbors counted off into clusters of fifty received their portion unquestioningly. The bread was chewy and soft, almost warm. The sardines were dried and salted perfectly. A day's worth of hunger took some minutes to fill, some minutes of grateful stuffed cheeks and eyes closed for the joy of food at just the right time. They ate until their bellies bulged, until they could eat no longer, and then they looked around at all the others—how merry this hillside was! New strong legs began to run and chase. Those freed from demons, and the once-leprous, ate dinner with their families for the first time in years. Was there ever such a meal?

The Twelve ate too, as hungrily as the others. They were too busy eating to ponder this, that the Master could multiply two dried and salted sardines as well as he could multiply fish in the sea. That the bread was halved and halved and halved and it just kept breaking into more. One of them, maybe James, remembered his words about not worrying what you will eat, that God will feed you at least as well as he feeds the birds. But mostly they ate, and their eyes were not opened. Even after.

When all had eaten, Yeshua was not yet done. He rounded up his followers and instructed them, "Gather the pieces that are left over. Let nothing be wasted."[1]

Did any of them protest, *What is the sense of this? When food is sparse, when resources are thin, when a god is limited and his miracles cautious and rare—yes, save every crust! Who knows when more is coming! But if someone has just filled every appetite—and can do it again and again, even then, "Let nothing be wasted"?*

What does he mean? Don't waste anything that Jesus has given and multiplied? Yes, of course! And what has he not multiplied in my life, in all of our lives? Over dinner that night, our fish camp table is heaped with two platters of deep-fried holy bottom fish, with green salad, quinoa pilaf, and two loaves of crusty whole grain bread. We sit before the table, salivating. We grab hands, ten of us. Duncan prays, "Thank you, Lord, for your provision every day, but especially today for this halibut. Be with us the rest of this day. Help us to do our work well." And we're off. Three forks head for the platter of fish. The boys are stuffing their mouths, barbeque sauce and salsa are passing, and everyone is filling their plate again and again while we laugh and the iced tea melts and brownies bake in the oven for dessert.

I sit at the table with these faces around me—my children, my husband, our crewmen, and friends—we pass the plates to one another, and I marvel. Duncan and I stumbled upon the beach of this island almost three decades ago, from another island, a place we had lived for ten summers. We came here, to this island, an island with two empty shacks and no one and nothing else. Before this, I came from five thousand miles away, from my own growing-up houses ruined and cold, with little heat, from tables where food was hard to find and doled carefully to each plate and there was no more. No one could enter these houses, because there was no food to share. I didn't know about miracles. I didn't know about Jesus. I learned to work hard, but there was never enough. I held on too tightly to whatever I had.

And somehow, despite our own limitations and small faith, God multiplied the work of our hands on this island, bringing forth a well of pure water beneath our shovels, building a house from our bent backs, as we carried every piece of wood, every window and table and matchstick up that long, steep hill that one long winter. Out of nothing but hope and muscles and prayer, through storm, darkness, and snow, a house emerged from our hands. Then, after more ardent prayers, children came one by one, filling this house, this island, until it throbbed with more living than I knew was possible. Could anything be better? Who needed anything more? And yet there is more. Out of the overflow, I began a writers' workshop a few years ago, with fifteen writers coming from everywhere to Harvester Island, harvesting words, multiplying images, stories, books, prayers. An island hillside that once drowned in fish, isolation, loneliness, and even death has become a place of love and art and feasting and life. Never could I have imagined such abundance!

But it's so easy to waste it all. Even knowing where and who it comes from is not enough, because the story is still not over. John's Gospel tells us what happened after the miraculous meal. Through the meal, the masses recognized him as "the Prophet who is to come"![2] They were so moved they chased after him. Not to thank him or to worship him or to join the disciples but to "force him to be king." Who wouldn't? Had I been on that hillside that day, I would have joined them in their collusion to capture Jesus and crown him by force. *You're the One! Be our*

King! Give us our nation back! Feed us every day! Take away our want!

But they are wasting it, this meal, this sign. They only want his food and his power; they don't want him. They want supremacy, not humility. They want their nation, not his Kingdom. Later, some from the hillside find him and confront him. Jesus identifies himself clearly to them as *the bread of life, come down from heaven to give life to the world.*[3] He tells them *he* was the manna that came down from heaven each day to feed the Israelites in the desert. The question they have been asking ever since, every time they say the word *man ha*, meaning "what is it?", has been answered. That bread was him, feeding them, sustaining them. And he has just done it again on the hillside. He wants them to know that he has come not just to feed them lunch but to be their life. But they reject him. They turn away, unbelieving, though their bodies are healed and their stomachs are full.

I know how this happens. Who does not want the bread Christ feeds us sometimes more than Christ himself? Which bread feels more real? I look around my table. Look how filled we are! I am so in love with all that Jesus has given me, too often I want only that. But take all this away—no children, no husband, no beauty, no sea, no tables full of halibut and bread—and will I love him still, this Christ? Can I trust him to be enough? When God's own prophets are killed, when Jesus sleeps through storms, when people we love drown in ocean or flames, can he truly be all we need?

The bread basket passes again. I reach in. There is one crust left. I pick it up carefully. I chew it slowly, not wasting a crumb.

CHAPTER TEN

OVER
THE WATERS

Then Jesus made the disciples get into the boat and go on ahead
to the other side of the lake, while he sent the people away. After
sending the people away, he went up a hill by himself to pray. When
evening came, Jesus was there alone; and by this time the boat was
far out in the lake, tossed about by the waves, because the wind was
blowing against it.

Between three and six o'clock in the morning Jesus came to the
disciples, walking on the water. When they saw him walking on
the water, they were terrified. "It's a ghost!" they said, and screamed
with fear.

Jesus spoke to them at once. "Courage!" he said. "It is I. Don't
be afraid!"

Then Peter spoke up. "Lord, if it is really you, order me to come
out on the water to you."

"Come!" answered Jesus. So Peter got out of the boat and
started walking on the water to Jesus. But when he noticed the
strong wind, he was afraid and started to sink down in the water.
"Save me, Lord!" he cried.

At once Jesus reached out and grabbed hold of him and said,
"What little faith you have! Why did you doubt?"

They both got into the boat, and the wind died down. Then
the disciples in the boat worshiped Jesus. "Truly you are the Son of
God!" they exclaimed.

MATTHEW 14:22-34, GNT

It's August 10. We've had glorious weather for an entire week, but not today.

"I don't like the look of that wind, Isaac. Let's hurry up and leave before it gets worse." I turn from the front window where I've been eyeing the waters with binoculars. It's just a seven-mile run up to the village to take Katherine to the mail plane. She's been with me for a week, one blessed week with another woman at the table. In my daily walks, in all my work ashore, and in the skiff as well. Since Naphtali left home for college a decade ago, with five sons and then crewmen besides to work with, I am always outnumbered.

Isaac glances out the window, shrugs. But even from here, I can see the southeast wind picking up down the bay. It'll be a wet trip.

"Katherine! Be sure to line your box and suitcase with plastic. We'll put it in the tote to keep it dry, but it looks like a nasty ride."

She emerges from the living room, her eyes questioning.

"It'll be all right. But if you miss this flight, Kath, you'll miss all your connections back to Virginia. They said they're flying, so we need to try to make it. Put on all your rain gear. Everything."

Katherine, who is beautiful, with black hair and enormous green eyes, nods quickly. Our week together has refreshed both of us. Thirty-eight years ago she was in my wedding, but after graduation, we lost track of each other. We didn't reconnect until a few years ago. In college, we were both English majors and we were both from the East Coast, but more, we shared a deep love for language, literature, and theology. We discovered to our delight, these decades later, that all of this bound us still.

"Isaac, we need to hurry!" I shout as Katherine and I head down to the gear shed to suit up. We'll put on all the gear we use for fishing: rubber knee boots, bibbed rain pants, life jacket, full heavy-duty rain jacket with hood and brimmed hat.

In ten minutes the skiff is loaded and we are off. I'm nervous. We're late. I don't think we're going to make the plane.

Isaac is driving. I would rather drive, but it's a man thing, I know. It leaves me free to sit beside Katherine. The first mile is good. The skiff rides the gentle chop with a light bounce. It's only blowing maybe twenty miles per hour. Then we come around the next corner, and a blast of wind hits us, and just keeps slugging. In less than a minute, the water has turned white, the waves are piling seven feet high with the wind whipping the tops off into the air we are trying to breathe. The skiff plunges into each trough and shudders as it rises over each crest. Katherine clasps the side of the skiff, and between the slashing spray flashes me a look of fear. I nod my head slowly and blink my eyes with a small smile, signaling, "It's okay. We're going to be fine." We cannot speak. The wind is too fierce. Whole sheets of spray are washing over us. We're perched on a single metal bench seat in the stern, but the pitch of each landing nearly unseats us. Katherine reaches an arm out for me; I cinch my other arm around her to help hold us both upright. I realize it looks like we're going to die. It looks like there's no way we're going make it through the next four miles of this hurricane water, but I know we will. I trust these skiffs, how seaworthy they are, all the water mountains they've climbed. As long as the motor doesn't die, we'll be okay.

In such a storm as this, would I ever leave the boat? We cling to the railings of the skiff, each of us, and cling to each other as we ride these wild waves. The boat is our only hope. It has floatation in the bow and in the stern. Even if it's half-filled with ocean, it can still float for a while.

In a storm, no one ever leaves the boat. A boat is an ark against the deep, a piece of land over water, your only hope. Unless—unless the boat is going down. I've never had to abandon a boat, but Duncan has. One night he hitched a ride to Kodiak on a friend's fishing boat. Around midnight, still ten hours from town, the fifty-eight-foot boat began to flounder in the dark waves. Unknown to them, the hatch in the stern had been knocked off by the lash of a wave, and slowly the stern filled with water, until it was too late. The boat pitched with such angles, Duncan and the two others knew it was going down. The skipper scrambled to the radio, sent off a "Mayday" over and over. With fear and shouts, in the panicking dark, they threw their survival suits on and launched the life raft. Yet even then they were not safe. The boat was nearly on its side by then. As they pushed away from the listing boat, ready to sink at any moment, Duncan knew the life raft could be snagged in the mast and rigging as it tipped and sank. They pushed off with a furious heave. Just minutes later, as the tiny orange life raft rode the night waves, the waters swallowed the boat whole.

They did not have long to wait. Another fishing boat heard their Mayday, diverted course, and picked them up a few hours later in the black of night. Wet, exhausted, they stood shakily but grateful on another deck, safe.

I know another man who abandoned his boat one harrowing night. That night, after a long day, after the hillside of thousands finish their banquet of bread and fish, Jesus sends his men ahead of him across the water. The crowds have left, now filled. The disciples are returning to Capernaum. But Jesus wants to stay. He can finally be alone. There is mourning to do—John. His cousin. He knew him from childhood. Grief itself multiplied in his chest even as he divided the fish in his hands. Long into the night he prays and weeps and sleeps when he can.

But the night is far from over for the Twelve. After all of these events—John dead, the thousands made well and full, the baskets they carried away—they just want to go home. They just want to sleep and get away from all the crowds and be normal, for a day or two. I know that's what they all want and need and expect. But no. The wind comes, like it comes to us on the waters so many times. A full, fierce howl that sends them leaning and pitching into their oars, moving nowhere at all that unending night. For nine hours they fight the sea with only their backs and arms. They wrestle the sea as they've never wrestled before. And surely the sea is going to win. They still have three miles to go but their strength is gone. They don't want to be fighting for their lives. They don't want to be in this boat, but they can't swim in these waves. They want to be home with family, safe, warm in their beds. There is only one place worse than where they are right now—out of the boat. In the water itself. Which is more than just water. It's more than just a sea. It's the abyss, a place that the Hebrews long feared, a place of monsters and ghosts, a place the dead fitfully inhabit. If nothing else, they still have each other—and the boat.

We know what happens on this night. Just before light, Jesus goes to them. He doesn't take another boat. He doesn't swim. He doesn't fly. He walks. Where is he stepping? Are the crests of the waves sloshing over his feet? I don't know. But they see his figure in the storm and scream in terror. It's a phantom, a ghost! Come up from the depths, from the abyss! They know it! They know all the stories!

Jesus hears their screams and in the wail of the wind, shouts back, "It is I!"

So convinced are they that he is a phantom, only Peter can muster a response. "If it's you, tell me to come to you!" he aims above the wind, his eyes wild.

"Come!"

And Peter does it. With that one word he does the unthinkable. He puts his hand on the rail and launches out over the smooth wooden side, the cradle that carries them safe from the drowning waves. The other men nearly drop their oars to see him leap into the storm. Peter has lost his mind!

But there he is! Peter starts off *atop* the waters, walking toward Jesus! Until he sees the water and feels the whipping wind about him. Panicked, drowning in his fear, he begins to sink and calls to Jesus for another water-rescue, and it's given. Jesus grabs Peter's hands, raises him up from the deep, and they both step into the boat. The moment they settle on the seat, the wind stops.

The men can hardly speak. They have seen Jesus go under the waters, they have seen him call down the waters, now they see him over the waters. Just months ago, when he flattened the sea with three little words—*Peace, be still!*—they were heartsick with wonder and fear. Shaken and breathless, they asked, *What kind of man is this?* They could only ask, they could not answer. And now they have their answer, this second time in the storm waters of Galilee. Do they see? He is the "I Am" who spoke from the burning bush before Moses. He is the One from Psalm 104:7:

"At your rebuke the waters fled." He is the one from Job who "tramples down the waves of the sea."[1] They collapse at the bottom of the boat. They are floating now, calm, safe.

I have not seen him walking toward me in the watery storm, nor have I climbed out of the boat to meet him. But I met him in a storm one day as surely as Peter met him on the water.

It was early June, our first week at fish camp. I was in the house, unpacking the piles of boxes, supplies for the summer, when I heard a wail of distress. The oldest then was fifteen, the youngest seven months, so I knew all too well the various symphonies of Upset: the wailing, the fussing, the he's-picking-on-me kinds of complaints and yowls. But this sound was different. I stepped out of the house and began walking down the gravel path, looking for the source of the sound, my heart already beating too fast. Then I saw him. It was Noah, thirteen, lying on the ground, writhing in pain. I ran to his side, tight with fear. His face was deeply abraded, blood everywhere. His nose looked broken. There was a puncture and another possible bone broken by his eye. His lower leg looked fractured. I saw the ATV at the foot of the hill still running and knew what happened. His first ride of the summer. He had ignored our helmet rule and had lost control while going down the steep hill. He had smashed into a tree—with his face and leg bearing the brunt of the impact.

I seized Noah's hand in a near-panic, spoke soothingly to him, *You'll be all right, Noah*, and in the next breath began yelling, "Help! Someone! Anyone! Come here! Help!" Duncan came charging from the warehouse. The kids came running. In less than a minute all were gathered around Noah, horror on their faces. "Get blankets!" I ordered them. It was about forty-five degrees and the ground was cold. Duncan bent down to take a quick assay of his injuries, then dashed to the house to call the Coast Guard. Naphtali, fifteen, came and sat by his head, singing and comforting him as he moaned. But what next?

I looked out around me again. We were in the third day of heavy fog. I could not see more than five feet beyond the beach into the water. Not a breath of wind stirred. No planes had been flying, no boats running for three days. No one could move, trapped by a smothering hand that nearly stole our breath as much as our sight. How could even the Coast Guard fly in this? I knew they wouldn't, but we had to try.

They answered our call immediately. But our guess was right. They could not launch a helicopter in zero-zero conditions.

Of course not. I knew it. I knelt on the ground next to my battered son, feeling crazy with fear. Noah was still conscious, but for how long? And what was the damage? What would we do if we couldn't get him to a hospital? I was angry as well. I was angry at Duncan for bringing me here those years ago. I was angry at myself for following him. Why did I choose this life, this work, this summer home, with its isolation and danger? The nearest hospital was sixty air miles or a hundred boat miles away. Not a great distance—unless the skies and the waters are doing what they so often do around Kodiak: strand us. Ground us. Keep us stuck. What was I doing raising kids so far from a hospital? Two of them I brought out as two-week-old newborns. The others all flew out as infants as well. How could I keep them safe? I had control over nothing. I looked around for God in the fog. I could see nothing but Noah's pain and my fears.

While Duncan was radioing the Coast Guard on their emergency channel, someone else was listening in. Dean Andrews, who ran Andrews Airways, a small bush plane company, heard the emergency call. He did not hesitate. He launched his Cessna 206 on floats and took off into the wool-thick air. Rather than flying across the interior of Kodiak Island, all razor-steep mountains, he flew the coastline, eyes on his instruments and on the coastal cliffs to guide him.

The usual thirty-minute flight to our island took an hour and a half, the longest hour and a half of my life, as we tried to keep Noah awake and to ease his pain. Naphtali continued to sing. I stroked his hand and kept praying, though I wondered if God could hear me through the fog.

The plane finally came—emerging out of some invisible closet. Within minutes, Noah was strapped onto a door to keep his head and neck still, then carefully lifted onto the floor of the plane. Dean, standing calm, looked at us. "Who's going with him? I only have room for one."

"I'm going in with him." I said it as a fact. I was not going to leave Noah, no matter what Duncan said. He saw the look in my face, nodded: "I'll stay here with everyone else." My going meant Micah as well: He was seven months old, my beautiful blond boy, and still nursing. I climbed into the back of the plane. Duncan handed Micah in the infant seat up to me. The row of two seats behind the pilot had been taken out, leaving just enough room for Noah and now me kneeling beside him on the floor with Micah, his seat on my other side.

We took off. On the floor, I could see nothing out the small pane windows but white. I concentrated on Noah's face, keeping him awake. The ER at the hospital told me to do this.

"Okay, Noah, we're going to do the alphabet. I'll start and you say the next letter. A."

Noah turned his head away, closing his eyes.

"Noah, you have to do this! You have to stay awake! What comes after A?"

"B," he said weakly, eyes fluttering.

It was a torturous trip through the letters, and we started next on counting backward from one hundred. Just as we hit the eighties, ten minutes into the flight, the plane pulled up hard, banking a desperate right angle, then straight up, flattening me to the floor. I knew what it was. *A mountain. We're going to hit a mountain.* I stretched out a trembling protective arm to steady Micah in his seat, another arm over Noah, my teeth clenched under gravity's fierce pull. This was it. This was my worst nightmare. The children I was entrusted to protect and keep safe were now going to die. I could do nothing about it. The hedge of safety—is there really such a thing?—I had prayed for around my family and our home had failed, twice this day: with Noah's accident and now this disastrous flight. I had failed my children. And God had failed us.

But it was not over. Something happened in that moment. I did not have a vision, but he was there. He was with us in the plane, in the fog. He had found us. I was sorry and sad for Duncan and all the others because they would not know this— that just before the plane crashed, we were with him. Perhaps just as Wanda was safe with him in the fire, and Dave's father and son in the waters of the bay. Even John as the sword came down. My heart was profoundly calm. I closed my eyes, one hand on Micah's tiny foot, and another on Noah's chest, and waited for the end.

We missed the mountain that day. The plane rose until it felt like we had hit heaven's door, and then the engine let go. We leveled out and picked our slow, painful way to town, around every cliff and pinnacle, the only plane in the air for a hundred miles. Noah was on crutches the rest of the summer. He healed from his injuries, with just a few scars to remind him.

But neither story, mine nor the disciples', is over because Jesus was not done with his people. "O you of such small faith!" he chides Peter as he sinks, horrified, into the waters. But I'm not sure that he chastises Peter for sinking in the waves. Peter's not supposed to be walking on water. He has a boat. He's supposed to be in the boat. I've read this story wrong for too long. We love Peter's impetuousness. It warms our heart, this passionate fisherman who, crazy with faith, leaps into the storm. This follower of Jesus who wants to imitate whatever Jesus is doing, a true *talmid*. And surely yes, we all must take leaps of faith into the scary unknown at times, but Jesus never asked him to get out of the boat. Leaving the boat wasn't Jesus' idea. Peter leaps over the side into the maelstrom not out of faith—but disbelief. Peter cannot believe that Jesus is there with them in the storm. Peter cannot believe that Jesus is who he said he is that night over the churning sea, though he reassures them three times! "Take courage!" "It is I!" "Do not be afraid." In response to Jesus' voice and his clear identification, "It is I!" Peter shouts back, above the wind, "*If* it is you . . ." He leaps out of doubt, not faith. He walks atop the waves anyway for a few steps, but fear opens his eyes and ears too wide. He hears the wind; he feels the water at his ankles. He knows this is impossible—and he sinks.

I think Jesus scolds me too in my own plane of a boat that

day. Because I did not see him until I knew we would die. I should know better. He has been with me all these years and still I miss him. Still I am blind to his presence in so many ways. In the midst of feasting, I am afraid of loss. In a gale, I see ghosts, the height of the waves, the lash of the wind. My faith is over-shadowed by fear and storm and even by satiety, but he comes into my narrow heart anyway. He makes room and enters when I think I am dying, and only then do I see him. Only then do I believe his love for me. And this is what I must do, what we all must do—see him as fully in the living as we do in the dying.

Even in the dying they did not see him that night. Nor did they see him in the bread that very day. That afternoon they carried away those baskets, each of them with his own reed basket full of Christ's bread broken for each of them, personally, and their hearts were hard, the Gospel of John tells us. They didn't recognize what was happening, that the bread he was feeding them with was himself, that he was soon to give his own body for the life of the world, for the life of each one of them.

They wanted bread, all right. The kind that fills your belly, but not the other kind. They thought their problem was hunger, not an appetite for power and revenge. They thought their problem was political oppression, not their own slavery to sin. That night, they thought their problem was the storm, not their blindness to Jesus' presence and love. They thought their problem was impending death, not disbelief.

But he comes to them anyway, and they are so not expecting him, they cannot believe it is him even when he identifies himself. Even when he says his name to them: "It is I"—the "I Am!" They have themselves seen his mastery over the water, but still they are expecting a ghost more than they are expecting

Jesus. They are believing in their own folklore, in a phantom, more than they are believing in Jesus. They are believing in their fear of the deep more than in Jesus. They do not yet know that he is with us wherever we are, that he will even walk on water in the middle of the night in a storm to come to us, that nothing can keep him from us, nothing can separate us from his love, not the present nor the past, not wind or waves or fire, neither height nor depth, neither living nor dying. *Nothing* can separate us from his love.

But they are beginning to know. They are beginning to see. Wet, panting, exhausted, they answer their own question that day when his voice calmed the sea: "Who then is this, that even the wind and sea obey him?"[2] They answer it now aloud and in their hearts again and again, huddled, soaking to their skin, as bone-weary from rowing as though wrestling with an angel all night: "Truly you are the Son of God!"[3] They say it in submission, in wonder as they bow before him, now safer than they've ever felt before.

The danger is over, though other storms will surely come. Jesus has come not to save them from the waters—death is not the enemy—but to save them from unbelief and their still-small faith. They don't know yet that Jesus is about to enter the biggest storm of all—death. And he will save them by himself, leaping into the waters we cannot swim. He will be the better Jonah, thrown overboard into the deepest seas and tallest waves, and he alone will overcome it. He will trample the sting and the storm of death.

I felt it that day, and I knew the question that stung at our feasting table last week was answered: If Jesus takes away all that he has given, is he enough? Kneeling on the floor of the plane, my blond-haired baby on one side, my bloodied, half-conscious son on the other, speeding toward the mountain, I knew the truth. My faith fell away, no longer needed. *Jesus*, I whispered through a clenched jaw, with closed eyes. I was ready to sink, to shatter, to fall, to rise into the One I had always hoped was there—*and he was*. And he was more than enough.

CHAPTER ELEVEN

UNFOLLOWING JESUS

Now when they had kindled a fire in the midst of the courtyard and sat down together, Peter sat among them. And a certain servant girl, seeing him as he sat by the fire, looked intently at him and said, "This man was also with Him."

But he denied Him, saying, "Woman, I do not know Him."

And after a little while another saw him and said, "You also are of them."

But Peter said, "Man, I am not!"

Then after about an hour had passed, another confidently affirmed, saying, "Surely this fellow also was with Him, for he is a Galilean."

But Peter said, "Man, I do not know what you are saying!"

Immediately, while he was still speaking, the rooster crowed. And the Lord turned and looked at Peter. Then Peter remembered the word of the Lord, how He had said to him, "Before the rooster crows, you will deny Me three times." So Peter went out and wept bitterly.

LUKE 22:55-62, NKJV

I CAN'T BELIEVE THE SIZE of this king salmon. It's three feet long and probably forty-five pounds, as thick as my waist. It shines on my kitchen table with the glint of the sun through the window. I know what I'm going to do with it: I'm going to smoke it. There's no better smoked fish than king salmon.

Over the next hour I strip it all out, notching the thick flesh to better absorb the flavors, then lay the meaty chunks into the white tub, already tasting its smoky-sweet goodness. When I am done, nearly an hour later, I call the two younger boys.

"Abraham! Micah! Come here, please!"

I yell three more times before they come. Their friend Caleb is with them for the week, a rare treat. The three come running.

"Hey boys, grab the carcass in the box there and toss it over the cliff. But not the box. Put that in the burn pile."

"Sure, Mom!" And they are off, impatient to fulfill the chore and get back to their play.

Five minutes later, they storm into the kitchen, laughing, poking one another, and hand me the basin, now empty, and race off.

"Thanks, boys!" I smile at them, with the basin in my hands. Then suddenly I look at the empty basin, and then down at the box at my feet with the carcass in it. My eyes go wide, my face flames. Disbelief erupts into shouts.

"Boys! Boys, come here!"

They hear my tone and scramble back, eyes questioning. I hold out the empty basin and then signal to the box.

All three of them freeze, their faces flush.

I try to control my voice and speak slowly: "You dumped the salmon over the cliff instead of the carcass." Then I give up all pretense of control. "Do you know how long I worked on that fish? How could you mistake the meat for the guts and the carcass?" With every word my voice gets louder.

Micah and Abraham are old enough to know any kind of defense is useless. They stand there hanging their heads, awaiting their fate.

That was six years ago. Ever since then, whenever I strip out a king salmon I am back in that moment, but my face no longer burns. I smile usually. I'm there now, working on two salmon at the kitchen table, preparing to brine them for the smoker. This batch is for Elisha and Isaac. They're leaving August 25, in just a few days. The summer is nearly gone. Part of the life of this house will go with them.

Sometimes loss and departure seem the summation of my life out here. That same week that the boys threw the salmon over the cliff, they mistook a box of all my research materials for a box of garbage. Into the fire it went, books and papers and notes, all I had amassed over a couple of years for a new book I was working on.

Must we always be called to relinquishment? I think of Elizabeth Bishop's poem "One Art": "The art of losing isn't hard to master; / so many things seem filled with the intent / to be lost that their loss is no disaster."[1]

Years before that, when Duncan's fishing boat went down, I lost my wedding ring, all my childhood journals and poems, every piece of paper that I held valuable and was trying to keep—sunk to the bottom of the sea somewhere out there in the Shelikof Strait. I am well practiced in this art. Who isn't? I have not lost dreams, because I never learned to dream, but

I've lost people. I've lost love. I lost my father, who could not say, "I love you, Leslie," not even once. I've lost family members through estrangement, beloved friends through distance and disease. And early this summer, just before I left for fish camp, I lost someone who was like a mother to me. She wouldn't let me come to see her. I didn't get to say good-bye before she died. I've kept myself busy and distracted these summer months, but some days my grief nearly sweeps me away. Today is one of those days. And soon, I will lose my children.

Last night, around midnight, I went down to say good night to one of my sons. We talked a long time. About how hard it is to grow up working for your parents. How hard it is to keep doing what you've done since a small child. How lonely he is here on this island without his friends. Yes, he loves us and is glad to be with us, but he longs to leave and make his own way out in the world.

I know, I know. I shook my head in understanding. I know how hard it was working for my parents, too, rebuilding old houses throughout our childhood. I know how tangled the roles get in every family business, how the children can feel like employees rather than sons and daughters. How, when we're working, our worth feels measured by our productivity. How so many of the words spoken between you and your parents are commands, and it does not matter how hard or impossible the work before you, it must get done. I know, too, about isolation from friends and the rest of the world. We all feel it.

I turn back to the salmon now and carefully place the last layer of fish on top. The basin is full now. I move it to the refrigerator on the porch, where it will sit until morning. I need to work in the studio, but I cannot write today. I feel a whirlpool of panic and melancholy sweeping me under.

I lift a sweatshirt off a hook by the door and walk halfway down the gravel path. Three skiffs are out on the water, loading ice from the iceboat for the afternoon pick. I'm already traveling through decades, across islands, a continent, while on it goes, the orange rain-geared soldiers marching down the hill, stepping wearily into skiffs and roaring out onto the nets. Come hell or empty nets or high water or any other thing, the fishing goes on as if nothing else matters. Yes, this is the constancy of need and the persistence of love, but it is slavery, too. Maybe that more than anything.

I feel a familiar vertigo. I am desperate to leave, but there's no way off this rock. All I can do is walk. I decide to visit the eaglets, to see if they're still in the nest. I set my face to the meadow and the only passable trail on this jungle of an island. I lurch down the graveled trail and turn toward the studio, the house that Duncan built for me a few years ago, where I do all my writing and where the writing workshop happens. I carefully chose this spot, tucking the white two-story building into birch trees overlooking the inside of the bay. I didn't want to face the outside waters, the Shelikof Strait. I see and remember too much on those dark waters.

What were we doing in those early days? We pitched our whole lives to following and catching creatures themselves headed for death. Part of me died too along the way. I had a miscarriage in the skiff one terrible day—and after going ashore to clean up and change, I went back out, back out into the boat to work into the dark. Because the men asked me to; they needed me and I could not say no, though a life had just been lost. It felt like my own life that night. Then the nights of driving a nearly swamped skiff around the island in the pitch dark near a reef I couldn't see; the week I took Duncan's place in the skiff, my breasts leaking milk while I battled the fall storms; the days of fishing until I could no longer stand but I wasn't allowed to sit, and we were crazy, all of us, arms going numb at night, hands unable to hold a cup, jumping from a pitching skiff onto a rock, the fierce shouting, my own voice lost, my pen stilled, my eyes long past tears. Who could write or speak about this? Who would believe it? Until finally I did it, what I'm doing now—I walked away. Without a boat or a plane, there was no escape from this island, except at the lowest tide, when a spit of land emerged, connecting to a larger island. It was all wilderness, but there was a driftwood shack four miles down that beach, too decrepit for habitation. But not for a runaway. With a gun over my shoulder for bears, a backpack with food, a sleeping bag, and matches for a fire, I left the island, never wanting to return.

I didn't stay in the driftwood cabin for long, just three days. I meant to stay longer, but I couldn't. Now, as I walk, in the midst of these memories, I feel as though I am on trial and I am pleading my case. Who am I talking to? I look up. It's a rare cloudless sky this afternoon. How fitting today, that even the sky has been emptied. I pitch my pleas heavenward anyway.

I didn't give up, did I? And neither did Duncan. We left that island and came here. You know all we did here, how hard we worked! We dug our own well, built every one of these buildings! And the fish came and came, and the kids came—four in seven years into this huge, empty house! We were so happy to have them all! And we were done having babies. But you sent two more in my forties, and I couldn't do it! How could I raise a daughter and five sons out here with so much dirt and an outhouse and an old wringer washer and all those fish, and then two of us, off on our own islands of fatigue and work, too tired to speak and even to fight. And did you see me those nights when I ran out into the dusk looking for a way off, a way out, the nights looking for you, *for the Savior I chose, a Savior who I thought chose me too . . . but where were you? Why is it all so hard? Did you trick us? Where is this better life?*

I'm on the trail again, walking faster, eyes stinging through a near forest of hogweed. I remember that flight in the fog—how can I forget? I remember how near he came, but in these other storms, surely he was sleeping! Can't I wake him up and say, "Lord, can't you see I'm drowning?" My father is gone. My mothering friend is gone. And now one by one, my children are leaving. I know they must go! But when I look ahead, just ten years ahead, I see an empty table. I see this house, the banya, the basketball court, the trampoline, the swing set, the tree house, the kitchen table—I see it all deathly still, deserted. I will be mending nets on the beach with strangers hired to work for us. I will be cooking for other mothers' sons. I will be the boss lady. That's all. What has all this been for?

I stumble now on a salmonberry bush. Crows mock from the alders overhead. I shout "Haw!" and they scatter, grieving and harassing as they part. I watch them, wanting to shout at them, *I don't want suffering! I don't want to be meek! I want healing and blessing and power! I want my children to stay! I want my family restored! I want my family to accept me! I want Jesus to be the king who brings all our daily bread! But what you've given is not enough, Jesus! You come in the storm, but you bring the storm! The bread is a stone, after all; the fish is a serpent—you tricked us, Jesus!*

And that's all it takes to put me there in the garden that night. I am a woman walking alone on an island in faraway Alaska, but I am there at Gethsemane that night. Maybe I am the one pointing the soldiers toward the path to the garden. Here they come with their torches and handcuffs, and they arrest him, this one I have tried to follow all these years. They haul him off in chains. They should. He is not who he said he was. He is not who I thought he was!

They run that night, all of the disciples except one. In the light of the torches, in the flash of the swords, in the terror of seeing their Master chained like a villain, they scatter like seeds on the wind.

This is not what they signed on for. They know what they need: the Romans overthrown, their nation restored, the Temple worship reinstituted, the return of YHWH to live with his people, his chosen, called-out people! And then he came, this Anointed One! They knew the new life would be better than the old life, and it was. It was for so long! They knew they chose well. What they saw! Peter saw him on top of the waves, on the hillsides feeding everyone, on top of the mountain, his face aflame with heaven itself. They saw the enormity of his power, the magnitude of his compassion, his fearlessness against his enemies. Yes, this is the King who has come to bring the Kingdom of God. Here he is! The One we've been waiting for! And they themselves, paired up, walking village to village, touching shriveled hands and leprous bodies and watching the fingers come back, the fresh skin appear—in *his* name! In his power!

Finally, just when they understand, just when they know who he really is, they come—the soldiers, the torches, the arrest, maybe death? Yeshua saved them so many times! From the storms, the crowds, the Pharisees. He can heal anything, anyone! But why is he not resisting? Why is he letting them shackle him and drag him off? Why doesn't he save himself?

Peter did not hear the dozen times Jesus told him, told all of them what was coming, that he would be mocked, whipped, that he would suffer and die. We don't hear those kinds of words when we're young, in the early days. We have no idea, any of us, what lies before us when we raise our hand, when we choose the ring, when we throw down our nets or pick them up, when we step on the island, when we sink under the waters, when we bow our heads. We don't know what will come of our yes, our "I do's," our "I will's," but we believe in those words. We believe in ourselves and our ability to keep them. I believed, when I was younger, that I would always follow Jesus, without question or pause. That night, Peter, sniffing the threat of violence, burst out passionately to Jesus, "I will go to the death for you!" Have I not said the same? But when the ring cracks, when your children leave, when the wrong kingdom comes, when the baby dies, when soldiers appear in the night with flaming torches, when one of your very own betrays your Master with a kiss—of course they ran!

Later that night, when Peter crept into the courtyard where Jesus was being held, the words of denial came just as easily as his pounding flight: *I don't know him. I don't know who you mean. Man, you're wrong!* And Peter curses just before the rooster cries his morning dirge. Jesus, across the courtyard, fixes his eyes on Peter's, and somehow he sees me too, and we are sobbing, both of us, Peter and I, as Jesus is taken away in chains. We're done following him. He's no king at all. We're saving ourselves, we are nursing our disillusions, we're giving up. We didn't lie in that courtyard, on that trail of grief and memory. We *don't* know him! He's not who we thought he was. But we know who *we* are. We are the seeds choked out by thorns. We are the bad fish thrown into punishment. I should have stayed in that driftwood cabin and fallen with it into the sea. Peter wants to take it all back—the leaving, the following. I want off this island and out of this life. It's a bust, all of it. We followed the wrong man.

Where is your power now, Jesus, Son of God? Where are your disciples now, rabbi? We are on our feet, trembling, and running away, all of us. *I told you that day to leave me! I said, "Go away! I am a sinful man!" Why didn't you listen to me? You chose us, and you chose wrong. We chose you, and we chose wrong. You are not who we thought you were.*

Man, we do not know you!

CHAPTER TWELVE

THE FINAL CATCH

Afterward Jesus appeared again to his disciples, by the Sea of Galilee. It happened this way: Simon Peter, Thomas (also known as Didymus), Nathanael from Cana in Galilee, the sons of Zebedee, and two other disciples were together. "I'm going out to fish," Simon Peter told them, and they said, "We'll go with you." So they went out and got into the boat, but that night they caught nothing.

Early in the morning, Jesus stood on the shore, but the disciples did not realize that it was Jesus.

He called out to them, "Friends, haven't you any fish?"

"No," they answered.

He said, "Throw your net on the right side of the boat and you will find some." When they did, they were unable to haul the net in because of the large number of fish.

Then the disciple whom Jesus loved said to Peter, "It is the Lord!" As soon as Simon Peter heard him say, "It is the Lord," he wrapped his outer garment around him (for he had taken it off) and jumped into the water. The other disciples followed in the boat, towing the net full of fish, for they were not far from shore, about a hundred yards. When they landed, they saw a fire of burning coals there with fish on it, and some bread.

Jesus said to them, "Bring some of the fish you have just caught." So Simon Peter climbed back into the boat and dragged the net ashore. It was full of large fish, 153, but even with so many the net was not torn. Jesus said to them, "Come and have breakfast."

None of the disciples dared ask him, "Who are you?" They knew it was the Lord. Jesus came, took the bread and gave it to them, and did the same with the fish. This was now the third time Jesus appeared to his disciples after he was raised from the dead.

When they had finished eating, Jesus said to Simon Peter, "Simon son of John, do you love me more than these?"

"Yes, Lord," he said, "you know that I love you."

Jesus said, "Feed my lambs."

Again Jesus said, "Simon son of John, do you love me?"

He answered, "Yes, Lord, you know that I love you."

Jesus said, "Take care of my sheep."

The third time he said to him, "Simon son of John, do you love me?"

Peter was hurt because Jesus asked him the third time, "Do you love me?" He said, "Lord, you know all things; you know that I love you."

Jesus said, "Feed my sheep. Very truly I tell you, when you were younger you dressed yourself and went where you wanted; but when you are old you will stretch out your hands, and someone else will dress you and lead you where you do not want to go." Jesus said this to indicate the kind of death by which Peter would glorify God. Then he said to him, "Follow me!"

JOHN 21:1-19

IT'S ALMOST OVER. I leave Israel tomorrow. I finished the hike around the lake yesterday just before dinner. I didn't walk far, but it felt momentous anyway. How should I celebrate? I stood in the Jordan River two weeks ago, with tiny fish nibbling my feet clean, but I want to do more. Instantly I know: I'll go back to the river, where I saw canoes to rent. I'll paddle out of sight and slip out of the boat into the river. I want to go all the way under. This is my last chance.

After lunch, I arrive on foot at the canoe rentals at the end of a dirt road. There it is, the river. My last look for a while. I frown. It's thicker and greener here than at Yardenit. I know why: There are no baptizing bodies here to aerate the water. I blink hard. Do I really want to do this?

I stumble a few more feet, avoiding some chickens, and find a hut with a young woman standing behind a wooden counter. She looks friendly. I approach her, smiling.

"Hello! Can I rent a canoe?"

"Yes. But are you alone?" she replies in near perfect English.

"Yes, I'm alone."

"Oh, I'm sorry, we can't rent canoes to anyone by themselves. For safety reasons." She points to a large sign I didn't see with a long list of rules, including the one I am now hoping to violate.

I look again at the river, which doesn't seem to be moving at all. "It would be pretty hard to drown in that."

"Yes, but that's the rule. You have to have another person with you. Insurance requires it."

I'm not giving up. "I live in Alaska. I run boats out on the ocean. In storms. Sometimes by myself." She looks at me, unmoved. "The waves are this high sometimes." I raise my hand over my head. "And you're not going to let me out on that little strip of water?" I'm never good on the other end of absurdity.

She shrugs. "Okay, let me make a call and check for you."

"Thank you." I have to go. Surely they will say yes. There are no other customers. I'll just paddle around that bend and then I'm free.

I hear her speak in Hebrew. Then she listens, nods, hangs up. "I'm sorry. It's insurance. If you had one more person, even a baby, you could go."

"I could go with a baby, but not by myself?" I repeat.

"That's right. Crazy, yes?" She raises her eyebrows empathetically.

What more can I say to her? I want to tell her what I know about the gathering of waters. I want to tell her I have changed my mind. I *do* want to be baptized again, but there is no one to plunge me under. After these weeks in the Holy Land, I see I am no different than the other pilgrims who come from across the ocean, over continents, following Jesus here to where he was baptized, where he walked, healed, ate, died, and came alive again. I watched men and women filling jugs with river water, bathing their faces in the sign of the cross. We all want to be cleansed, forgiven, set free, but do we all remember it is not the water that does it, but Jesus himself? I have seen him there not in the river, but in the weeping, singing, worship, in the splashing, the supplication, the need.

Maybe this is what Jesus saw too that day he walked beside the shore not far from this very place. Maybe this is why Jesus chose those fishermen and later the others. I am certain he did not choose the fishermen because they already knew how to sail a boat or cast a net. No one was chosen because of his possible utility. No one was chosen because of his experience, his background, his skills, though surely all of them had skills and intelligence to bring to their discipleship. Nor has he chosen any of us for any of those reasons. Jesus chose them, I think, for a simple reason: They were looking for him. In the midst of their busy fishing life, they were among the first to go down to the river to John the Baptist.

I am not surprised by this. Fishermen are thirsty. Fishermen are needy. Fishermen live by faith. The priest at St. Peter's chapel beside the Sea of Galilee was right. No matter what kind of nets are used, and no matter whether they're dropped in the ocean, in a river, or in a lake, fishing is always a supreme act of faith. Every day is a gamble. We learn all we can about the waters, about our gear, about the fish. We work from morning until dark for months. But in the end, we have no control over what comes. We have no control over the weather, over the water, over the fish. We cannot catch a minnow without him. We wait upon God. Every net that is thrown into the water becomes a prayer: *Give us this day our daily bread.* Sometimes our nets are filled to sinking. Sometimes they are blank. But we keep on praying. We keep on seeking. We are bent toward supplication. And Jesus always finds those who thirst and seek. Those who know they can do nothing on their own.

I was not a fisherman when Jesus first found me, but this life on these shores has bent me low and strong. Even now, this last morning on the nets. I'm still raw from my runaway walk a few days ago. But I'm feeling better. Our fishing summer is nearly over. In less than a week the writers will be here for the workshop. Soon we'll all be gathered around words, art, food, prayers, beaches, and whales. Then back to Kodiak for the winter, and my trips to the Lower 48 to teach and speak. Pure grace.

The weather has turned. I'm wearing two sweatshirts and a down vest today—the wind is cool. The leaves on the birches have already turned, and the fireweed is out in brilliant pink. The hillsides glow in their new fall colors. Duncan is here, Abraham and Micah, Peter and Josh are on the other side of the net. I've just finished my first big hole. I'm happy to be nearly done with the nets for the year.

"Micah!" Duncan calls now into our mending silence. "I need you to bail out the other skiff on the beach."

Micah looks up from the webbing in his hand. "Is that the really dirty one?" He looks around to see who knows.

"Yeah, it had a lot of jellyfish in it," Peter answers.

Micah groans. "Do I have to?" He looks at me, pleading. "It stinks! I can smell it from here!"

I can smell it too. But I'm not letting him out of this.

"Micah, you just need to do it. Abraham did it last time."

"Does anyone have a gas mask?" he shoots. He's wearing his favorite clothes, a pair of red sweatpants with holes in the knees, a striped sweatshirt and lime green crocs held together with duct tape.

"Here." I take off the blue bandana I'm wearing and hand it to him.

Resigned, he drags over to the beached skiff, tying the bandana around his nose. I glance at him while I mend. He empties a few bailers of sludge, then I hear a muffled shout.

"I can't do this!" Micah stands leaning over the skiff sides.

"It's not that bad!" I call back. In the next moment I hear

him retching. He's out of the skiff, bent over on the sand, vomiting again and again.

I close my eyes. When I open them, he is sitting on the beach, head down, shaking his head. "Sorry, Mom, I just couldn't do it," he says to me weakly as I approach. My heart and stomach melt. I remember one year, one storm when Abraham and Micah went missing. In the house. They were eight and ten years old. It was blowing thirty-five miles per hour, and it was time to go out on the nets. Duncan started calling for the boys, but they didn't answer. Everyone began looking and calling for them. For twenty minutes. But they were hiding. They tucked themselves under a bed and held their breath until the thunder of feet and voices subsided, and everyone trudged down the hill and out into the white waters without them. Duncan wasn't planning to take them out into that storm that day, but they didn't know that.

Micah is still breathing hard, his face red. He looks at me. "I can't finish, Mom."

"It's okay. I'll do it," I say quietly as I sit down beside him, though I am already feeling nauseous at the thought of it. I stroke his back. *What are we giving you, my son? Strength, I hope, and love, even in the midst of blows and jellyfish.* I want him to know the love of Jesus, to know that it's tangible, real. What have my other children gained from this life? Courage, I know—a fearlessness that has taken them far away, into other countries, into theatre, chemistry, business, teaching. They will at least come back to visit, they assure me. I have to let them go, no matter how I feel. They have work to do in the world, just as I do. And I am not alone! Katherine was here. The writers are all coming next week! I remember a few summers ago a woman kayaked to my island, knocked on the door—broken, guilty. We sat over coffee and the Bible, sharing our stories and tears. God keeps bringing people to my doors.

I give one last touch to Micah and turn to the beached skiff, resolved. I take a deep breath of cool salt air, pull my turtleneck up over my mouth and nose and step into the boat. The stench nearly knocks me over. And it's pink, I see. The jellyfish soup, up to my booted ankles, has turned to pink vomit both in appearance and smell. I immediately repent of my earlier judgment of Micah. I try not to look as I bend low to scoop. One scoop, two, I'm on my third when I have to breathe. Before I know it, I'm retching too, bending over the railing. Finally the retching stops. I turn back to the slime. Eighteen bailer dumps later I climb out of the skiff, walk to the water's edge sucking in clean air blast after blast. I stand for a few moments, shuddering.

"Are you okay, Mom?" Micah calls from the nets.

I wave my arm and answer without turning around. "I'm fine!"

I *am* fine, though I cannot help a rueful smile as I scuff through the sand back to the nets. When I came to this new country, I had no idea how sunk I'd be in flesh and fish. In rot and death. Nor could I guess what lay before me when my just-born babies were laid in my arms. When we follow Jesus and fall under the waters, we soon discover that faith doesn't sweep us out of the world. We don't escape the diapers and dirt; rather, we get clean to get dirty again. We rise to immerse all the more in this dusty, mucked-up, beautiful world where love and bodies and sacrifice twine through every moment. Love calls us deep into the guts of the world.

The disciples, though, aren't there yet. At this point in the gospel story they haven't emerged; they're still under the waters of loss and confusion. Their Messiah, their so-called Messiah, ended up staked out on a bloody Roman cross, like all the other rebels before him. They repented then of all of it. It was all a tragic mistake—leaving their families, leaving the nets, those whole three years of following this man. They're finished. They have no idea what has just happened. They don't know yet that everything they hoped for has come true. They don't know yet that God came not to save his people *from* storm and suffering but to save them *through* storm and suffering. Israel *is* redeemed. The temple—Jesus himself—*is* restored. Rome's power *is* defeated. The Crucifixion was a crowning. The burial was a planting. The Kingdom is here. God *is* with us!

But right now they are broken and they are hungry. Six of them climb into the boats that night. It's Peter's idea. Fishing is a risky business, with no guarantee of return, but they still have their nets, they still have their arms and strength, their knowledge. Simon Peter knows the sea. He knows the fish. And he'll be faithful to the sea, at least. He'll be faithful to his friends and the other fishermen. The other men will see—he can be trusted. They all ran too, that night, but he was the first. Yeshua had trusted him. *No wonder he died*, he thinks. *He trusted the wrong people. And we, too, trusted the wrong man.*

It wasn't enough for them to see the risen Jesus. They had seen him twice by then. They could not speak for the wonder of it—alive? Real? They had touched him, his hands, the wounds by his feet! But he didn't stay with them. He'd appear, and then disappear, leaving them again and again. They were alone now most of the time. Alone, yes, together. They had formed unbreakable bonds with one another—who else knew where they'd been the last three years? But the Master wasn't with them like he was before. He had abandoned them just as they had abandoned him. But the sea will hold them, and the fish with their blank eyes see nothing. *Set the net again, brothers!* Peter calls.

Do you see them out there, laboring all night, with the lights blazing and the two boats coordinating the nets, and haul after haul—nothing? Not a single fish to sell or cook for their own breakfast! Their utter destitution on the water that night is a mirror image of their souls. They have nothing. They can catch nothing. They cannot catch even a minnow on their own. Whatever skills they thought they had are not enough. They remember another night when this happened—three years ago, when it all started. They all think of it, but no one speaks. What's the point?

Just before morning breaks, just before they give up, a man calls to them from shore (*Who is it? Can it be?*). Hesitant, they do what he says (*Nets dropped on the other side—again?*), and in one impossible moment their nets are full of the biggest fish they've ever seen. Don't they know this pattern—a man speaks and out of nothing, out of dearth and failure explodes this crazy unending abundance? Peter sees him clearly now. He throws on his clothes and leaps into the sea. This time he thrashes toward the Lord instead of begging him to leave.

All the men are around the fire now. It crackles with a homey warmth on the sand. The fish lie in baskets ready to be taken to the market. This is the third time Yeshua has come to them, but they cannot speak. They are more confused than ever. Yeshua was tortured and brutally executed. And now he's alive, filling our nets again, filling our stomachs? Abundance still, even after death? What is this?

The food is nearly gone now. The fire settles. A plume of smoke follows the wind and hovers over one cluster of men, then another. Then Jesus speaks.

Simon, son of John, do you love me more than these?

Peter startles. Yeshua, sitting on the other side of the embers, looks straight at him. His face is quiet and kind. Simon Peter looks around to see what Yeshua means. He looks at the sea, the boats, his best friends, the fish on the sand waiting to be sold. He blinks, dazed. He knows the truth now. None of this is his. None of this can feed him. Then he looks back. *Yes, Lord, you know that I love you*, Peter stammers. This is the first time he's spoken to the Master since that night. He pants with relief.

Yeshua blinks, smiles at him, tilts his head, and asks again, *Do you love me?*

Peter freezes. Yeshua isn't asking, "Will you ever turn from me again? Will you ever make a mistake again?" His question is for me as well, because I was there too that night. *Do you love me?*

But he asks already knowing the answer. He knows Peter's mind and heart already; he knows my heart already, but Peter, distrusting himself, does not know until it bursts from him.

Lord, you know *that I love you!* In saying it, Peter knows he does love this now-risen Messiah enough even to die for him. And he will. Simon will die for the name and the sake of Jesus years later. Jesus tells him how he'll die in another few words. But now, one last time, the only question that matters:

Simon, son of John, do you love me? Jesus asks quietly, in a low voice, with unwavering eyes.

Peter flinches. Why doesn't Yeshua believe him? *Yes, Lord, you know that I love you!* He nearly shouts this time. And just as he speaks, he hears it. I hear it. Three questions. Three answers. Is it possible? Is it possible that his every denial is now forgiven, covered by love? By Yeshua's love for him, and incredibly, his own love for Jesus—his own small, limited human love? Our love is enough, then?

Peter would never forget this exchange. He would go on to write to the early church, and to all believers after: "Above all, love each other deeply, because love covers over a multitude of sins."[1]

This is the gospel right here, in these words around this fire. Peter is forgiven of his faithlessness, his selfishness, his fear. And I am as well, and every one of us who has ever run away from the One who is our very life. Because this is the truth of following. When he said, "Come, follow after me," it also meant that he would come after us. We have nothing to offer him. We stumble, we faint, we run the other way, and still he comes after us. He wants us. He loves us. He does not let us go.

But Yeshua is not done. This is not just about us. Every declaration of Peter's love is met with a charge:

Feed my sheep.

Feed my lambs.

Take care of my sheep.

So, Peter's love is enough. And this love has work to do out in the world. As we have been fed, as we have been forgiven, let us feed others. Others where? Everywhere. Later Jesus commands, "Go into all the world." Can this be? I want to protest, say back to Jesus, *Do you know how weak we are, how wavering our faith, how limited our love? Are you really trusting us? How can we do this?* And I know the answer has already been given. Through the fish. Through the wine at the wedding. Through the bread on that hillside, and in so many other ways. He is the God who takes whatever we bring to him—our destitution, our tiny faith, our two small fish, our very human love—and multiplies it beyond measure. God will make our love enough.

Jesus calls Peter one last time into this new world: *Follow me!* Must he leave the nets again? Yes, because Peter is *still* a fisherman, as his retreat to the boat and the nets reveal. But Peter is so much more than a fisherman now. And I am as well. He never leaves us as we are. These eleven uneducated men will go out into the world, fearlessly crossing land and sea, establishing the church, leading others into this new Kingdom, this new country of forgiveness, abundance, and love. The waiting is over. God has come to live with his people.

What about me? What can I claim, that I have followed this Messiah, my Lord, perfectly, or even well? I still stumble along a meandering path. And I likely always will. I still mourn my children leaving. I battle pride and selfishness. I wrestle unworthiness and shame. I ask a hundred questions: Why couldn't my father love me? Why did Wanda die in a fire? Why is there so much suffering in the world? Why did my mother-friend have to die so soon? But he has done more than I could have imagined that day in the church basement when I raised my hand and said, *Yes, Jesus, I give you my life.*

I asked him to lead me, and so he has. But now, after all these pages, I'm not sure I came to this Alaskan island following Jesus. After this watery trip all of us have taken, I realize I came here myself. I chose this country myself, though I hardly knew what I was choosing. But through this place he has led me further into a new land I could never have imagined or reached on my own, a place where a father can be loved and forgiven, where a house and table are filled with many sons and daughters—mine and others', where a marriage rises from the ashes again and again, where a ragged wounded family learns to reconcile, where a mother sacrifices for her son in the skiff, where a plane in the fog misses the mountain, where fishermen stand mending nets while praying for brothers and sisters around the world. This is a holy place. This is heaven. This is God with us. God with us in all of it, in the storms, in the fish, in the doubt, and in all the seas. I am no longer afraid.

And I pray he is with us in these pages as we've crossed these waters, as I've tied and knotted this web of words. They are as tangled and as imperfect as I am, but love compels me. *Feed my sheep*, Jesus commands. I cast this net out now, hoping to feed any who hunger, hoping to catch all who seek. He is calling. Do you hear?

Come, follow me.
Do not be afraid.

DIVING DEEPER

HERE WE ALL ARE, stepping into this boat together. Maybe you've followed Jesus all your life, maybe you just met him for the first time, maybe you don't know much about him at all but are wondering what this Jewish man from long-ago Israel has to offer you. We're all in different places, and yet we're all in the same place. We face storms, and doubt, and fear, and we wonder how we're going to get through. We wonder if we can trust this man sitting on the anchor or walking across the water or teaching things we don't understand—and calling us to follow.

He is here, with us, and he's asking us to follow him into deeper waters. And even though that seems scary, *is* scary, he's worth the trust. Worth the risk.

This study guide is a way for all of us to dive a little deeper into what this book talks about. We're wandering through Galilee and crashing over waves in Alaska and talking to the disciples, and what does it all really mean for us—for me—for you? That's what this guide is the beginning of. I've included research and thoughts and questions to help you navigate your own waters, whatever they may be. So come on, step into the boat. You might be surprised what Jesus has for you on the other side.

How to Use This Study Guide

As with any journey, there are a variety of paths you can take through this study guide. Personally I'd recommend reading the whole book through, gaining the broader picture of Jesus and what it means to follow him, and then approaching this guide with the fuller sense in mind. If you're more of a linear type, though, you may want to go through chapter by chapter, engaging with each story and conversation and aspect of following as you go along. Go through each chapter at your own pace. Soak in the stories, underline the things that jump out to you. Put yourself in the disciples' shoes. Imagine yourself in my knee boots in Alaska. And as you go through the study, grab your favorite journal and write down your thoughts about each of the questions. It's important to write these things down. You never know what God wants to remind you of later on.

If you're using this guide as a personal study, make sure to sit with the stories, the truths about Jesus, the realities of us. Don't hurry through. God may have some insights here especially for you.

If you're using this guide in a small group, commit to building personal, meaningful relationships with the others in your group. Because, again, we're in this boat together. Our perspectives, no matter how different they are, can help clarify one another's storms. Respect each other. Listen to each other. Love each other.

Tips for Group Leaders

This study guide has twelve sessions, making it accessible for a small group seeking a twelve-week study. If you are facilitating this guide in a small group, here are a few tips:

- As much as possible, get to know your group. Recognize that everyone is wounded in some way. Set a tone of grace and trust for people to share their doubts and hurts. Be sure to share personally from your own life as well, so you don't come across as the only one who's "got it all together." Remind the members of your group that we're not here to fix one another's lives or edit someone else's story. Only God can do that.
- Start and end with prayer. You can pray, or ask others to pray, but don't force anyone to pray who may not feel comfortable. This needs to be a safe space.
- Encourage group members to read the chapter prior to each meeting. While the questions are intended to spur discussion whether or not someone has read the chapter, group members will get the most out of the discussion if they spend time in that week's chapter.
- At the start of each study session, consider asking members to identify passages they found particularly meaningful or provocative. This will refresh everyone's memory of the chapter as well as serve as an overview for those who missed reading it.
- Each session has five questions. This is intentional. We're all busy, and it's important for group members to engage with a few specific questions rather than get overwhelmed and not be able to engage. Some questions encourage group members to go deeper into Scripture, and some lead group members into more personal reflection. Allow people to speak when they feel comfortable. Depending on the amount of time you have, and how open your group is to discussing, you

may want to focus on one or two specific questions and go deep in those.

- Before you begin your first session, ask your group to commit to creating a healthy group context. As facilitator, ensure this continues throughout the study. If one person continues to take over the discussion, gently redirect to allow others to speak. Encourage introverts to be involved in the discussion, but don't pressure them if they feel uncomfortable. And make sure everyone agrees to respect confidentiality within the bounds of the group.

I'm glad you're willing to dive deeper into these waters with me. Let's brave the waves together, knowing Jesus is walking beside us all the way.

THE GATHERING
OF THE WATERS

GOD'S WORD IS SATURATED in water. Before the earth was created, before even light and dark, sun or moon, before any creatures existed, there was water (Genesis 1:2). Water is one of the most potent metaphors and symbols in the Scriptures, appearing 722 times in the Scriptures, sweeping us all the way from Genesis to near the end of Revelation.

It's not difficult to understand why. Water is essential for all of life, of course, but beyond this, the Israelites wandered through deserts and inhabited a desert land where the scarcity of water then amplified their concern and focus. Most people settled along rivers and oases, and dug wells for access to this precious commodity.

Just as water is essential for all life, so God is essential for all life—which is probably why he so often used the metaphor of water to describe himself, his character, and what he values most:

- He describes himself as Israel's fountain of life-giving water in Jeremiah 2:13.

- In Isaiah, water is a simile for the knowledge of God: "As the rain and the snow come down from heaven, and do not return to it without watering the earth and making it bud and flourish, so that it yields seed for the sower and bread for the eater, so is my word that goes out from my mouth: It will not return to me empty, but will accomplish what I desire and achieve the purpose for which I sent it" (55:10-11).
- In Hosea the rains are a sign of the presence of God: "Let us acknowledge the LORD; let us press on to acknowledge him. As surely as the sun rises, he will appear; he will come to us like the winter rains, like the spring rains that water the earth" (6:3).
- In Amos water represents social justice: "But let justice roll on like a river, righteousness like a never-failing stream!" (5:24).
- Again in Isaiah, water is the promise of blessing and renewed life: "But now listen, Jacob, my servant, Israel, whom I have chosen. This is what the LORD says—he who made you, who formed you in the womb, and who will help you: Do not be afraid, Jacob, my servant, Jeshurun, whom I have chosen. For I will pour water on the thirsty land, and streams on the dry ground; I will pour out my Spirit on your offspring, and my blessing on your descendants" (44:1-3).

Sometimes we can take water for granted, can't we? Turn on the tap and it's there. Grab a bottle on your way to work. Turn on the shower. It's only in the moments we're confronted with it—fighting the stormy deluge or feeling the rushing water over our toes on the beach or experiencing drought—that we pay attention.

But maybe, if water is so important to God, we should pay more attention.

1. Reexamine Jeremiah 2:13; Isaiah 44:1-3; 55:10-11; Hosea 6:3; and Amos 5:24. What positive attributes of water, and positive associations with water, do we see in these passages?

2. Put yourself in the shoes of the people these prophets were speaking to. What would they have heard and understood about scarcity of water? How would that have impacted their understanding of these words?

3. For my first ten summers in the Alaskan bush, I carried all our water for washing and cooking in buckets from a well up a hill and then up two sets of stairs. Because it took so much energy and time to get it there, water was a precious resource I never took for granted. So when I read these images of flowing waters as a sign of God's blessing and abundance, I feel the truth of it deeply. What memories come to mind when you think of water? What role has water played in your life? How might your experience of water connect with your understanding of God?

4. Maybe you're approaching this book with a lot of doubts. Maybe you're new to following Jesus. What do you struggle to understand about who Jesus is? What are some of your questions and doubts as you begin this study?

5. Perhaps you have been a believer in Jesus for a while. As you start this book, what questions do you still have about following Jesus? What challenges have you faced as a follower of Jesus?

UNDER THE WATERS

THE EXCITING EVENTS IN THIS CHAPTER—John's baptizing of penitents in the Jordan River and then Jesus' baptism by John—signal the beginning of something radically new for the Jewish people. And for us two thousand years later.

For the Hebrew people, John's baptism carried weight and associations from their past: Their people were figuratively baptized when they passed through the Red Sea. So we shouldn't be surprised when we find John the Baptist down by the Jordan River, bringing people through the Jordan, symbolically reenacting the Exodus.

John called people to a baptism of recognizing and confessing sin. But if baptism is for penitents who are turning from their sin, and if Jesus is without sin—why did Jesus insist on being baptized? There are several possible answers:

1. Jesus' baptism was an anointing, revealing his identity as the divine Son, King, and Messiah.
2. He was asserting his own high priesthood by undergoing the Jewish cleansing rite for priests (Leviticus 8:6).

3. He was identifying with sinners and symbolically enacting the bearing of humanity's sins under the waters of death. Later, in his death on the cross, he would fulfill that symbolic enactment.

Baptism is a profound moment for each of us today as well. We follow countless other believers into the water, going under the waters of death, which we deserve because of our sin, and then rising up into new life, cleansed of our sins because Jesus has paid for them in our place. As the Israelites walked through the Red Sea and toward God's Promised Land, we go through the water and enter into a new relationship with God: "Once you were not a people, but now you are the people of God" (1 Peter 2:10). As we saw from the previous chapter, water symbolizes life. In baptism God has also promised that he would do a new thing—and this is how he's doing it.

1. Read Matthew 3:1-11. What was the purpose of John's baptism? Why did he respond so harshly to the Pharisees and Sadducees who came to the baptism?
2. Read 2 Corinthians 5:17-21 and Romans 6:1-11. How was John's baptism different from baptisms done after the death and resurrection of Christ?
3. What is the role of baptism in our current church? How does it differ from the baptisms of John and the baptisms of the early church? How is it similar? Are there any ways in which baptism today should be approached differently?
4. Have you chosen to be baptized? If so, why? If not, why not?

5. If you have chosen to be baptized, what new thing has God done in your life since? If you have yet to be baptized, what new thing might he be calling you to through baptism?

CALLING OUT OF WATER

Among the Jewish people, Jesus was originally known as a rabbi, which means "teacher" or "master." We see people encountering Jesus, addressing him as rabbi, and asking him difficult questions about the Law. But the rabbinical system was not fully established until AD 70, after the destruction of the Temple. Only then did the position become formalized with an official educational process and subsequent office. In Jesus' day, rabbis taught the Torah in the synagogue, in synagogue schools, and to their disciples, but it wasn't necessarily full time, and the rabbi was often from the lower or middle classes. But despite the less formalized system, people still had clear expectations of a rabbi. Expectations that Jesus would challenge and upend completely—beginning with his practice of choosing his own disciples rather than the best students choosing him.

His choice of disciples was entirely unconventional. But not for the reasons we may suppose. We often think of the fishermen in the ancient Near East as coming from the lowest rung of society, but this is not accurate. Most fishermen were solidly middle-class, as were tax collectors. The fishermen disciples were part of an operation that included at least two boats and at least four men, including hired men. But even so, Jesus' choices were strange. Rather than choosing among the better-educated and more sophisticated Jews in Jerusalem, he chose disciples who were not well educated and who came from a place most considered the sticks. His other choices were equally unexpected. Some of the other disciples were politically risky. Matthew (also called Levi) was a tax collector; such men were despised by the Jews because they collaborated with their Roman oppressors. Simon the Zealot was a revolutionary, stirring up the peace, trying to overthrow the Roman government.

These are the ones Jesus handpicked. And we, too, have been called to follow, though most of us aren't among those we'd expect Jesus to choose—we haven't necessarily moved across an ocean for him, or devoted all our time to evangelism, or lived among the least of these. No, we are the ones driving to the office every day, cleaning up after our kids, maybe even, as in my case, literally holding on to our nets. And most of us are called to follow right where we are.

1. What biblical principles laid out further in the New Testament seem to be at work in Jesus' choosing of the disciples? (See 1 Corinthians 1:26-31.) How does Jesus' choosing of these men give us encouragement and hope today?
2. Jesus tells the fishermen they will soon become "fishers of men." They couldn't know what this meant, of course. But they followed and obeyed anyway. What does this example reveal to us about the nature of Jesus' calling?
3. Read Matthew 4:18-22 and Mark 1:16-20. Some believe

these passages illustrate God's "irresistible grace," meaning that when Jesus, in his sovereignty, calls, no one can resist. Others emphasize human choice. What do these passages lead us to understand about our response to God's calling?

4. Jesus called the fishermen from their nets to fish for men's souls instead of fishing for fish, but he did not call them from the world they knew. Later in John 17:15 he prays for his disciples, "My prayer is not that you take them out of the world but that you protect them from the evil one." In many ways, Jesus was calling them *more deeply* into the world and people's lives than they had experienced before. Have you experienced this similar kind of paradox in your own life as you respond to God's call? Explain.

5. The church has a long history of dividing the world into flesh and spirit, beginning with the interpretation of Matthew 4:18-22 and Mark 1:16-20: Jesus moves the disciples from fishing for fish to fishing for the souls of men. How do we understand this call today? What does it mean to follow Jesus in the midst of our flesh-and-blood everyday lives?

THE CATCH OF CATCHES

Can we hear how strange these words must have sounded to the fishermen? "From now on you will catch people instead of fish." This wasn't normal rabbi talk. The image of throwing out a net and catching people had to be unsettling, even ludicrous. Where does it say that in the Torah?

But what was normal about any of this? A rabbi choosing his students out in a boat, when everyone is covered in fish gurry, instead of in the synagogue, bent over the words of God? Those four fishermen couldn't have known what he meant, but right here, right from the start, Jesus was signaling something new. Something different. This was not a rabbi's usual pitch or promise to his potential students and disciples. Disciples were the sharpest students of God's laws and the Mishnah and Midrash, their traditions and interpretations of that law. Signing on to follow a rabbi meant becoming a more knowledgeable student. It meant they could better argue the fine points of God's Word. But this man, this Teacher, is promising something else. He says, "You *will* catch people." He's promising action, not just words and knowledge. He's promising that they will be a part of this action, whatever it is, not simply observers. And he's promising that their focus will be on others, not just themselves.

What did those twelve men expect when they signed on to follow Jesus? In Jesus' day, becoming the disciple of a rabbi meant primarily sitting under his teaching. It was unthinkable for a student to study Torah on his own. Rabbis were those who demonstrated a superior knowledge of God's law as well as the various interpretations and applications handed down through their history. The rabbi served as a kind of mediator between the students and the holy text, guiding the students in right understanding and application. The twelve men called into this unique relationship with Jesus expected to spend their time learning, memorizing, discussing the Scriptures under the wise tutelage of this rabbi. And they did indeed do these things.

But Jesus was not just asking them to enter into a student-teacher relationship. He was asking for far more. He was asking his followers to turn over their lives entirely to him. To give him everything they had, everything they were. But they didn't know this yet. They did know that the Greek word Jesus used for "follow," *akoloutheo*, means literally "to walk the same road." It implies companionship, partnership. They wouldn't have understood this yet, how their lives would be melded together out of love, far beyond a student-teacher relationship.

It's the same for us. Even when we raise our hand or feel our hearts yielding to Jesus, we can only grasp so much. Our faith and understanding start out small, and grow gradually over time as we learn more and more from Jesus, about this life of faith and what he asks of us. This makes the early disciples' response to Jesus' invitation all the more remarkable. They didn't know that much about him, but they knew enough to say yes, to drop their nets, to walk with him wherever he might take them.

Our "yes" to Jesus' call looks different for each one of us. Peter, Andrew, James, and John laid down their nets. Matthew walked away from collecting taxes. Mary sold her most precious possession to worship Jesus. But in many ways, despite these outward differences, the act of obeying and following is the same. We are each called to "lay down our nets"—meaning, to leave the familiar, the comfortable, to step outside the structure and security we're accustomed to and trust in the voice of the One who calls us. This doesn't mean that Jesus calls everyone to leave her profession or his hometown. But it means a profound change in inward direction. That instead of following our own desires, fears, and plans, we choose to entrust our lives to Jesus' plans.

We may not leave our profession. We may not pack up and leave our hometowns, but we're abandoning ourselves and our own human efforts as the source and direction of our own lives—choosing Jesus' path instead. And that always comes with a cost.

1.   What was Jesus demonstrating by filling the fishermen's nets with fish? Read Job 12:7-10. Based on this passage, why do you think the fishermen felt compelled to leave their nets after the greatest catch of their lives?

2.   Consider the fishermen's lack of knowledge of what they were following Jesus into. In your own life, if you have made that decision to follow Jesus, how did it happen? Was it a gradual growth of knowledge and understanding about the identity of Christ and his claim on your life,

STUDY GUIDE: THE CATCH OF CATCHES

or was it more immediate? What were your expectations then of this new life, this new relationship with Jesus?

3. For decades, many churches and denominations have described salvation, the new birth, as "asking Jesus into your heart," which describes an immediate response and submission to the person and call of Jesus. Is this different from following after Jesus, and if so, how? In what ways has the twenty-first-century Western church separated these two actions: belief in Jesus as the Son of God and then following him wherever he leads?

4. What are some of your questions about these events and Jesus' call to "follow"? What makes sense? What makes you feel uncomfortable?

5. There is always a human cost to following Christ. Describe some of the costs the fishermen must have experienced as they left the life they knew to walk beside Jesus for the next three years. What are some of the costs you have experienced as you've followed Jesus?

A FISH OR A SNAKE?

YESHUA SURPRISED HIS NEW FOLLOWERS at every turn. His first miracle, turning the water into wine, was not what they anticipated. And in Matthew 5:1-22, 43-48, Jesus continues upending expectations. He is announcing the beginning of the Kingdom of God—a new economy of abundance, seen in the provision of water to wine, seen in the mass healings and deliverances. But the people healed here are likely to get sick again, and they will all die. Clearly there is a twofold nature to the Kingdom of God: our present sufferings and our future healing and restoration. This would have been both good news and bad news to Jesus' listeners. As Jews under the heavy hand of Rome, they were waiting for a here-and-now physical deliverance through the Messiah.

We can take for granted, sometimes, his announcements about the Kingdom of God and who we are called to be in it. Many of us grew up reading about them, heard about them in Sunday school, nodded sagely as Jesus blessed the meek and the poor and the mourning. But consider with me the strangeness of it all. Jesus came announcing a new Kingdom, a new world. In that new world, Jesus had authority over all disease and suffering. He freely healed all who were sick and demon-possessed, giving all a taste of the coming Kingdom of Heaven, where there are no tears or mourning. But after the healings, Jesus taught them that blessing in this life here and now will look different from what we expect. We're blessed when we *don't* receive what we want. He blesses our many states of need instead of our state of fulfillment.

Don't we all want and expect fish instead of a snake? If we're following obediently, of course things will go well with us! Of course life will be easier! If God is with us, we're not going to lose our jobs! We're not going to get sick! Our kids are all going to love Jesus, and all will be well! But—maybe not. Jesus never comes to us or speaks to us in ways we expect. Sometimes the fish *is* a snake. What does that mean about our Jesus then?

1. Read John 2:1-11. What are some of the reasons Jesus' followers and the wedding guests must have been astonished at this miracle?
2. John writes, "His disciples believed in him." Yet we'll see in future events how small their faith was. What do you think the nature of their faith was at this point?
3. Read Matthew 5:1-22, 43-48. What teachings would have been particularly difficult for the listeners to hear?
4. What teachings here do we as a church seem to struggle with most?
5. We all want to avoid suffering, yet in this chapter we reflect that sometimes blessings and good come from unexpected difficulties. Looking back in your own life, how has God increased your capacity, endurance, and blessing through difficulty?

SESSION SIX

ROCKING THE BOAT

Parables were not entirely unknown to Jesus' listeners—the Old Testament presents a number of parables (Judges 9:8-15; 2 Samuel 12:1-4; Proverbs 23:29-35). We often think of the parables as simply an engaging way to teach. Jesus is universally acknowledged as a great teacher, after all, even by those who reject his claims to be the Son of God.

This chapter, however, reveals an interesting paradox. If Jesus is such an effective teacher, why then did so many of his listeners reject his message? There's a larger answer. Jesus did not speak in parables just to engage his audience. He wasn't simply telling stories of familiar places and activities because it was an enthralling teaching technique; rather, through narrative he was reshaping their understanding of their history, of their expectations of the Messiah, of even God himself. The parables depicting the Kingdom of God were often abrupt, even shocking to his audience, perhaps to unseat them from their deeply entrenched religious traditions and views. It seems, as well, that Jesus' parables were framed to require something from the listener—that they would have "ears to hear."

We are no different in our struggle to understand him, to believe him, to have ears to hear what he's actually saying. Perhaps we are also entrenched in our own religious traditions. So many of us have heard his Good News one way or another, and yet what kind of soil has that seed found in our lives? We can follow Jesus and still the seed struggles to take root in the face of pride or anger or fear. Do we, any of us, have ears to hear?

1. Read Matthew 13:18-23. What does it mean to have "good soil"? What things identify people who receive the seed of Good News and bear fruit?
2. Read Hebrews 4:12. What is the purpose of the Word of God? Read the surrounding context in Hebrews 4. Why is it important for us to hear and understand the Word of God?
3. How have you observed people respond to Jesus? What's the most common response? Why do you think that is?
4. What is choking out the growth of the seed in your life? What would it look like for you to have ears to hear?
5. If the seed of the Good News has taken root in our lives, if we have been made alive in Christ, our response should flow from the enormity of what God has done in choosing us. Does this joy and gratitude emerge in your life? If so, what does that look like? If not, why do you think that is?

MENDING THE WORLD

RABBIS WERE NOT SEEN AS PROPHETS, but clearly, one of the roles Jesus fulfilled was that of prophet. Prophets were called to speak God's words to God's people. The Jewish people recognized his prophetic role and often thought he was Elijah who had returned, as was foretold in the Scriptures. Because God's people had a long history of rebellion, the prophets' messages were often about judgment. Jesus' words were no exception. While many of his teachings were hopeful and comforting, Jesus *did* proclaim and warn about the coming of judgment for all those who do not respond to God's return to his people.

But in the last decade, among certain segments of the church there has been a considerable softening of the harder teachings of Christ, particularly on judgment and hell. Jesus, however, never shrank from teaching what he knew would be hard to hear. He was not interested in popularity; he was interested in speaking God's fullest truths. And if Jesus is who he says he is, then we cannot sort and parse out his words—what we want from what we don't want. Either it's all true or none is true. We either keep following—or we leave.

Jesus told seemingly simple stories that invited people in toward understanding, yet that also required faith to hear and to obey. He didn't force compliance. He didn't insist on obedience. He simply illustrated what heaven is like—and what judgment is like—enabling his listeners to see the eventual outcome of whatever choice and response they made. The same choices and outcomes are ours as well.

And if we struggle with Jesus' teachings on judgment, we need to realize that the reality of future judgment and hell is actually a force for peace and good here and now. God's coming judgment removes the need for our judgment against our offenders now. We can't judge rightly anyway—only God can judge perfectly. Only God knows people's hearts. We can step out of the cycle of violence done to us, knowing that God *will* make everything right in the end.

1. When Jesus spoke to the disciples about the purpose of parables in Matthew 13, he quoted from Isaiah 6. Read Isaiah 6:1-10. What was the context in which Isaiah heard these words? How does this further speak to the purpose of parables, particularly in relation to separation?

2. Read John 9, focusing in particular on verses 35-41. What does this text teach about the purpose of God's judgment?

3. Judgment, the idea that some people will ultimately pay for their sins, while we have been forgiven for ours because of the shed blood of Jesus Christ, can be uncomfortable to think about. What struggles do you have with the idea of judgment?

4. We all have judged others at one point or another, even if only silently. How does passing judgment on others

contribute to the cycle of violence in our world? What would happen if you chose to fight against judging others in your own life?

5. What situations or relationships in your life need mending? What can you do to work toward peace in those circumstances?

STORMING THE PEACE

THE SEA OF GALILEE is 696 feet below sea level and is banked by 1,000-foot mountains around part of it, causing sudden violent winds. The disciples were familiar with the danger of these winds. As fishermen, and even simply as travelers across the sea, they likely had been caught in them before, and they would have known, as well, others who had been swept up in the waves. So you can imagine their fear as the storm surrounded them.

Think about this storm from the disciples' experience and perspective. They've witnessed astonishing displays of Jesus' power: over disease, over jars of water, over demons, over fish of the sea! But—he's sleeping. *He's* sleeping through the storm. He *is* a man after all. But then, when the terrified men finally awaken him, he stops the storm. So—he's not a man. But why then did he sleep through the storm?

They question his love for them. Why are you letting us go through this storm? Why are we almost dying when you're with us? Aren't you here to heal us and save us and rescue and redeem us? You chose us and now we're dying?

We ask these questions too. Why this sickness? Why this death? Why this broken relationship?

When we choose our spouse—to follow each other through life—what do we expect from that love and that choosing? That we'll protect each other. That we'll always be with each other, as much as possible. That we'll always come to the other's aid.

Add the divine here: The One who has chosen us, and we've chosen back, has all this power! So if God is a loving God, how can evil or tragic things happen? How can bad things happen to God's people?

The fact that Jesus slept in the midst of the storm is yet one more clue, yet one more indication that the rescue Jesus was bringing the disciples was different than they thought. And it may be different from what *we* thought when we first were saved, first gave our allegiance to Christ, first said, "I want to follow you!"

When we go through a hard time—and we all go through difficult struggles—we often struggle with our faith as well. We're out in that raging storm. Is Jesus with us—or not? We can't see him. And even if he is, maybe he's sleeping.

But we can't lose sight of the fact that as soon as Jesus was awakened and he saw the fear of the men and the size of the storm, he ended the storm immediately. He chides them for their small faith—perhaps because they didn't wake him sooner? There's much to consider from this story, and all of it requires faith that God has a purpose in every storm. That there is likely a purpose even in Jesus' "sleeping" in the storm.

1. God's love in the storm often takes a form we don't expect. Read Zephaniah 3:17. What does this indicate about how God comes alongside us in our storms?

2. Why do we often wait so long to call on Jesus when we're in the midst of a storm?

3. David's cry in Psalm 22:1-2 comes from a very human place. So often we feel like God is silent no matter how loud or prolonged our cries for his help. And David's words—"My God, my God, why have you forsaken me?"—are echoed by Jesus on the cross, during the ultimate silence. What does God's silence while Jesus hung on the cross hint about his silence during our storms?

4. Have you ever doubted God's love for you? What brought you to that place? What brought you out of it?

5. Has God ever rescued you in a way you did not expect? What did this rescue look like? How did you respond?

FILLING THE HUNGRY

THE INCREDIBLE FEEDING OF THOUSANDS of people is the only miracle, aside from the Resurrection, reported in all four Gospels. Yet—in many ways, this miracle was wasted on the people. None of them understood what was happening. We often think of Jesus' miracles as being performed for the sake of God demonstrating his power and identity—as God. But many of the miracles Jesus performed did not lead to faith.

Miracles alone don't produce faith. The Israelites in the desert had been rescued miraculously by ten plagues and the parting of the Red Sea, yet just days after those events, they were faithless and complaining again. God fed them miraculously in the desert every day—but they stopped seeing this.

And for any of us, miracles are never enough, not because of any insufficiency of the miracle itself or of the One performing it—Jesus—but because of our own insufficiency, our blindness. If Jesus fed the people on the mountain to show them who he was, then his mission failed. The people responded by trying to wrest him and force him to be king over them. But God's miracles are not just to show us "this is how great God is"—but to demonstrate what life looks like in the Kingdom of God, where every action is motivated by love.

We cannot perform the miracles that Jesus does, but his love for us can motivate us to love others in similar ways. We may not be able to multiply food, but we can feed those who are hungry. We may not be able to heal the sick, but we can tend to those who are suffering. We may not be able to calm the sea, but we can comfort the hearts of those in the midst of the storm. And we may not have the power to raise the dead, but we can point others toward the life and love that has been given to us.

1. Read Matthew 4:1-11. Why does Jesus refuse to turn stones to bread to feed himself in the desert? Contrast this to the feeding of the multitudes in Matthew 14:13-21. What is the difference?

2. The disciples were more than observers in this miracle. What part did they play? What does this say about the part we are to play in God's work?

3. What do you think the twelve baskets of leftovers symbolized or meant? What "baskets of leftovers" has God given you that you might not be seeing?

4. What miracles has God performed in your life? How did they impact your faith long-term?

5. How is God calling you to be his disciple in action this week? What hope and life as a child of God are you able to bring to someone in your life?

OVER THE WATERS

IN 2013, a large stone mound was discovered under the Sea of Galilee very close to where Jesus walked on the waters out to the struggling disciples. One of the archaeologists who made the discovery posited that this enormous assemblage of basalt boulders just under the surface of the water provided a platform for Jesus to "walk on the water" to the disciples in the boat. And if the stones hadn't been in that precise position in Jesus' day? Well, then the archaeologist suggests that with adequate funding and scientific testing, "he would be able to say with confidence that Jesus did not walk on water at that site."[1] It's the logical explanation, right? To an unbelieving world, Jesus could have walked on water only if there'd been something for him to place his feet on.

But we too are always looking for ways to deny and discredit the unnerving possibility that Jesus was and is God and that he does indeed control all the elements of creation. Most of us aren't stupid, but we can be thickheaded and dull and slow to learn of Jesus' ways. Even those of us who have tried to follow him for many years make mistakes, miss him, turn to self instead of him.

The disciples' experience gives us hope. We expect to be able to trace a perfect line of growth for them. That an event would happen, Jesus would display his love and power, and the disciples would take note, learn, and then move on to the next level of knowledge. This usually didn't happen. The twelve men continued to be dull students. Not because they were stupid, but because Jesus was so utterly unlike any other person they had known.

The biggest threat we all face is not physical danger, but doubting God's relationship with us, doubting who God is, his character and his love for us. Jesus calls us not to believe in a set of dogmas, doctrines, though certainly there is substance to our beliefs. But he calls us to more; he calls us to hope and trust and believe in *someone*. He calls us into a unique relationship.

The Gospel of John gives an account of Jesus' water-walking as well. And John's story provides an intriguing detail: After Jesus identifies himself, "Then they were willing to take him into the boat, and immediately the boat reached the shore where they were heading" (6:21).

Is this another miracle, or did it just seem that Christ's comforting presence with them transformed their sense of time, and the miles and minutes flew by, delivering them to their destination? We know that Christ had the ability to transport the boat, disciples and all, to the other shore, but my sense is that the second scenario is more likely. When we are in relationship with Jesus, and when we "take him into the boat" on our stormy sea, the storm may not yet be over. But his presence chases away the doubts that steal our breath and our faith. Eventually, in a time of his choosing, we *will* reach the shore.

1. Read John 6:16-21. How is the "lesson" the disciples learned from this event different from the other storm experience?
2. Read Isaiah 40:25-31. Why is doubting God's relationship with us, doubting who he is, more dangerous than physical danger?
3. Our journey of faith is never a straight line. Like the disciples, we often don't see God's work even when it's happening right before our eyes. What is a work of God that you have seen only in hindsight? How does this strengthen your faith for the future?
4. What does it mean to "take Christ into the boat" in your current circumstances?
5. Too often we see God most clearly in those moments when everything else is stripped away. What are ways you can seek to see him "as fully in the living as we do in the dying?"

UNFOLLOWING JESUS

WE TEND TO LOOK DOWN on Peter, I think. *I don't know what you're talking about.* It's a bald-faced lie, on the surface, an outright denial of everything leading up to that point in the Gospels. But maybe, on the other hand, it wasn't a lie. Everything Peter and the other disciples had hoped and dreamed and planned for with this man Jesus had just fallen apart before their eyes. He was supposed to be the Messiah, the one to overthrow Rome, the one to rescue their people, and here he was, submitting to the murderous Romans? And when Peter fought back, ready to stand in the battle with his Messiah—Yeshua told him to put his sword away? Peter had promised to die with him, hadn't he? This was no Messiah, not the one Peter had been waiting for. *I don't know the man*, he responded to his questioner, adamant.

But Peter, unlike the other disciples, couldn't stay away that night. He had to know. Waiting, watching, wondering. And the more time that passed, the longer Jesus stayed a prisoner and moved toward crucifixion, the more vehement Peter's responses became: "Then he began to call down curses, and he swore to them, 'I don't know the man!'" (Matthew 26:74).

We have defined ideas of who Jesus is, the life he's called us to, what he's going to do in us and for us and around us—and when he doesn't? When we lose the job or lose our family or lose heart and he doesn't show up the way we thought he would? When we're ready to fight, ready to stand our ground, and we look over and he's not standing with us? *I don't know the man.* Like Peter, we have created Jesus in our own image. He's not the man we thought he was. We are crushed, disillusioned. Will we, too, "unfollow Jesus"?

1. Read Job 30:16-20. What was Job expecting God to do in his situation? What did he experience instead?
2. Read Job 38:1-11. Who does God say he is? How does this speak into Job's expectations?
3. When have you felt let down by God? What things were you believing about God in that situation?
4. In what ways might you be creating Jesus in your own image?
5. Sometimes we understand Jesus, and sometimes we don't understand him at all. How do you respond to this idea that the One we want to trust above all others is often unknowable?

THE FINAL CATCH

FOLLOWING JESUS IS NEVER what we expect. We'll go through times of trust and doubt and fear. We'll experience suffering. But we discover that despite the promises of the "prosperity gospel," God came not to save his people *from* storm and suffering but to save them *through* storm and suffering. In those times, Christ comes to us just as he did to the disciples in the storm-tossed boat. We are not always saved from physical death, but we are saved from ourselves, from our fear, from our disbelief in God and his love for us.

This final passage, this final catch, is one of the most hopeful and empowering moments in all of Scripture. Peter has made many mistakes in the last three years as a disciple of Jesus, but none worse than the night Jesus was betrayed. We've all been there. We've all denied Christ in one form or another. Is there any hope for us?

Jesus is so tender and gentle here. He *knows* Peter, deeply, just as he knows us. He knows what Peter needs and what we need. Restoration. Relationship. And incredibly, in the exchange between Peter and Jesus, Peter discovers he possesses the one quality needed most to continue serving Jesus: love. With this love, Peter is equipped to answer Jesus' new call to "follow." The Kingdom they are proclaiming, then, is far different from the one they expected. It's not a place of power and supremacy. It won't come through the sword. The Kingdom of God is a place of forgiveness, abundance, and love, all of which Jesus demonstrated again that day of the last miraculous catch of fish. The Kingdom is far better than Peter could have imagined.

Jesus comes to us, too, in our moments of doubt and wandering, and he calls us through them. But the forgiveness and restoration he brings to us is not for us alone. It is for the restoration of many others as well. This, then, is why we're to "follow him" out now into all the world: that we may live out the Good News of the gospel wherever we are. And what is the Good News? Not that the Kingdom of God is coming, John the Baptist's words, but that the Kingdom of God is here! God has come to dwell with his people. God is truly *with us*. How? Through the coming of Jesus and the salvation he provides, through the Holy Spirit, God indwelling us, and through his living Word. Yes, we will still face empty nets at times. But we know the Jesus who walks on water, the Jesus who calms the storm, the Jesus who multiplies the fish and bread and whatever we bring to him. This abundant life in Jesus is worth proclaiming. This Jesus is worth following.

1. Read Isaiah 43:16-19. What does God tell us about himself? What does he promise?
2. How has God saved you through the storm rather than from the storm?
3. Read John 21:15-19. What one quality qualified Peter to

undertake this massive job of founding the church? What does Jesus mean by "feed my sheep, feed my lambs"?

4. What are some ways that we are feeding God's sheep right now?

5. Read Matthew 28:19-20 and Mark 16:15. Peter and the other disciples did "go into all the world" with the gospel. Do we have to leave home to fulfill the Great Commission? What does "going into all the world" look like in your life?

NOTES

INTRODUCTION
1. Mark 12:30

CHAPTER ONE: THE GATHERING OF THE WATERS
1. G. K. Chesterton, *Orthodoxy* (Chicago: Moody, 2009), 92.
2. G. Reckart, "The Jewish Background of Christian Baptism," 1996, http://jesus-messiah.com/html/mikva-baptisms.html (accessed May 3, 2016).

CHAPTER TWO: UNDER THE WATERS
1. Psalm 72:8, NLT
2. Zechariah 9:10-11, ESV
3. Zechariah 8:3
4. John 1:22-23, NASB
5. Genesis 6:5
6. Isaiah 61:1
7. John 1:29, author's paraphrase
8. Mark 1:11, author's paraphrase
9. "Jordan," Behind the Name, http://www.behindthename.com/name/jordan (accessed May 3, 2016).
10. "Jordan River," *Encyclopaedia Britannica*, January 12, 2016, http://www.britannica.com/place/Jordan-River.
11. Luke 3:7

CHAPTER THREE: CALLING OUT OF WATER
1. Matthew 4:20

CHAPTER FOUR: THE CATCH OF CATCHES
1. Luke 5:8, author's paraphrase
2. Luke 5:10
3. Ibid., author's paraphrase
4. Mark 10:26, author's paraphrase
5. Mark 10:28, emphasis added
6. Mark 10:29-30
7. John 14:6, NASB

CHAPTER FIVE: A FISH OR A SNAKE?
1. Selections from Matthew 5:2-11, 44, ESV
2. Matthew 22:33

CHAPTER SIX: ROCKING THE BOAT
1. Mark 4:3-4, ESV
2. Mark 4:5-6, ESV
3. Mark 4:7, ESV
4. Mark 4:10, NASB
5. Matthew 13:10, author's paraphrase
6. Mark 4:13
7. Mark 4:14, author's paraphrase
8. Mark 4:9, author's paraphrase

CHAPTER EIGHT: STORMING THE PEACE
1. Mark 4:37, ESV
2. Matthew 8:24
3. Mark 4:38
4. Mark 4:41, BSB
5. Mark 4:40, ESV, emphasis mine
6. John 2:11, CEV
7. John 1:29
8. Mark 4:41, ESV
9. Matthew 16:24

CHAPTER NINE: FILLING THE HUNGRY
1. John 6:12
2. John 6:14
3. John 6:25-35

CHAPTER TEN: OVER THE WATERS
1. Job 9:8, NASB
2. Mark 4:41, ESV
3. Matthew 14:33

CHAPTER ELEVEN: UNFOLLOWING JESUS
1. Elizabeth Bishop, "One Art," *The Complete Poems 1927–1979* (Farrar, Straus and Giroux, 1983), 178.

CHAPTER TWELVE: THE FINAL CATCH
1. 1 Peter 4:8

STUDY GUIDE SESSION TEN: OVER THE WATERS
1. Karin Kloosterman, "The Mystery Mound Where Jesus Walked on Water?" Israel21c, August 25, 2013, http://www.israel21c.org/the-mystery-mound -where-jesus-walked-on-water/.

leslieleylandfields.com

Harvester Island
Wilderness Workshop

Off the coast of
Kodiak, Alaska

Harvester Island is a **wild,** stunningly beautiful place for **retreat, growth, community,** and **workshops.**

Leslie Leyland Fields
leslieleylandfields.com

Guest Writers have included Bret Lott, Philip Yancey, Gina Ochsner, Jeanne Murray Walker, Luci Shaw, Paul Willis.

"As a writer wanting help for his craft, I found the workshops to be good, enjoyable fun. And then the whole Harvester Island Wilderness added the intangibles: Fields' family hospitality, interesting people, food, bush planes, skiffs, wildlife, outhouse and banya. It all refreshed body and soul; I opened up, slowed down, and started to breathe again."
—Daniel Cecil

"Leslie, thank you so much for a superbly memorable week! Your and Duncan's gracious hospitality was more than I could have imagined! The information, ideas, friendships and wildlife brought much joy. My heart longs for Harvester Island." —Lynn Rowland